WHAT THE BELLHOP SAW

A COMEDY

By

Billy Van Zandt and Jane Milmore

SAMUEL FRENCH, INC.

45 WEST 25TH STREET   NEW YORK 10010
7623 SUNSET BOULEVARD HOLLYWOOD 90046
LONDON   TORONTO

IMPORTANT BILLING AND CREDIT REQUIREMENTS

All producers of WHAT THE BELLHOP SAW *must* give credit to the Authors of the Play in all programs distributed in connection with performances of the Play and in all instances in which the title of the Play appears for purposes of advertising, publicizing or otherwise exploiting the Play and/or a production. The names of the Authors *must* also appear on a separate line, on which no other name appears, immediately following the title, and *must* appear in size of type not less than fifty percent the size of the title type.

Please note:

Mention is made of songs which are *not* in the public domain. Producers of this play are hereby *CAUTIONED* that permission to produce this play does not include rights to use these songs in production. Producers should contact the copyright owners directly for rights.

Cover Photograph of "The Bellhops" by Danny Sanchez. (Clockwise from top: Billy Van Zandt, Art Neill, Eric Anderson, Glenn Jones, Michael Kroll)

What the Bellhop Saw opened at the Henderson Theatre, Lincroft, New Jersey, on Thursday, May 25, 1989. It was produced by Mark Fleming in association with Phoenix Productions and was directed by Mr. Van Zandt. Set design was by Bob Thompson. Scenic design was by William Lee. Lighting design was by Joseph Rembisz. Costumes were designed by Kitty Cleary. Technical director was Neil Murphy. Stage managers were Jennifer Milmore and Sharon McGoldrick. Sound was by Scott Wheeler. Posters by Chris Stone. Photography was by Danny Sanchez. House Manager was Kathleen Milmore. Box office: Margaret Nodes and MaryAnn Schulz. The cast, in order of appearance, was as follows:

WALLY	Eric Anderson
GEORGIE	Billy Van Zandt
MR. BICKHARDT	Michael Terzano
STAN	Michael Kroll
ROGER	Glenn Jones
MISSY	Jane Milmore
HEATHER	Mary Ann Smorra
GUEST	Michael Chartier
ARLENE	Sherle Tallent
BABU	Art Neill
LITTLE HEIDI	Jennifer Milmore
"NUMBER FIVE"	Bob Thompson

TIME

The Present

SETTING

A posh hotel room in New York City

ACT I

Late afternoon

ACT II

An hour later

ACT I

SCENE: A posh New York City hotel suite. A double-door USR leads into the hotel hallway. USC, a king-size bed is raised on a one-step platform with two nightstands. Two large windows are on either side of the bed. They are practical, leading out to a two-foot ledge through which we see a panoramic view of Central Park. USL is an archway from which we see the hallway leading to an offstage bathroom. An adjoining-room door DSL leads to a neighboring suite. DSR is a closet, in front of which sits a small table and two chairs. SL is a wet-bar and a bolted down T.V.

AT RISE: On a red-uniformed bellboy (Wally) entering USR pushing a cart. On top of the cart sits a bottle of champagne in an ice bucket and two glasses. WALLY wheels the cart into place. HE dances to the music which plays on the radio as HE goes about setting up the champagne bucket, and turning down the bed. There is a KNOCK at the door. Three short raps. WALLY climbs off the bed, remakes the spread, turns off the radio, and goes to the door. HE KNOCKS five times. The outside knock KNOCKS back twice. WALLY opens the door. In steps GEORGIE, a nervous accountant. He wears a drab suit, and carries a small overnight case.

GEORGIE. Wow!

WALLY. Anybody see you come in?

GEORGIE. No. (*Reacts to room.*) Wally, this is spectacular.

WALLY. Four hundred bucks a night. (*Off Georgie's reaction.*) Don't worry, Georgie. It isn't costing you a cent. Nobody knows you're even here.

GEORGIE. What if they book the room?

WALLY. They won't. I checked with security. They're keeping this room empty all weekend. No one's ever gonna know you're here. Unless the President drops in or something.

GEORGIE. He won't drop in, will he?

WALLY. I don't think so.

GEORGIE. But what if he does?

WALLY. I'll come get you. Relax, brother. This is all yours.

GEORGIE. And Heather's.

WALLY. Yes. And Heather's. What time is she meeting you here?

(GEORGIE opens his overnight bag and takes out a heart-shaped box of candy and a bouquet of

flowers. HE rests both on the bed and closes the empty suitcase.)

GEORGIE. Six o'clock on the nose. She's very punctual.

WALLY. What did you tell that bull moose you're married to?

GEORGIE. I said what you told me to say. I have to work late.

WALLY. Good boy. You should have done this long ago.

GEORGIE. I wouldn't have to sneak around like this if Arlene would just divorce me! But she says she wants the pleasure of seeing me miserable until I die an early death due to excess stress.

WALLY. But she has boyfriends!

GEORGIE. I know.

WALLY. And they wear your suits.

GEORGIE. I know.

WALLY. Then what are you sneaking around for?

GEORGIE. Cause Arlene is bigger than I am. Besides, I have to be careful with Heather. She's everything Arlene isn't. She's . . .

WALLY. Sexy?

GEORGIE. Yes. And . . .

WALLY. Intelligent?

GEORGIE. Yes. And . . .

WALLY. Funny?

GEORGIE. Yes. And . . .

WALLY. She doesn't reek of cod liver oil?

GEORGIE. Yes. Well, you get used to that, actually.

WALLY. Georgie Leach, this will be the romantic night of your dreams. (*Holding up champagne bottle.*) A little champagne. A view of the park. (*Dimming lights.*) Soft lights. (*Taking roll of electrical tape from dresser drawer.*) A roll of electrical tape.

GEORGIE. I sure hope Heather goes for this.

WALLY. Why wouldn't she go for this?

GEORGIE. Well, because she doesn't really know about it.

WALLY. What?

GEORGIE. I kind of told her she's coming here to take dictation.

WALLY. She doesn't know she's meeting you here for a mad night of animal passion?

GEORGIE. Not exactly.

WALLY. Well, what "exactly" does she think, exactly?

GEORGIE. She knows she's my secretary. And . . . that's about it, "exactly."

WALLY. She's worked side by side with you at Bendetson, Bendetson & Howard for three years and she has no idea how you feel?

GEORGIE. Not exactly.

WALLY. Does she even have a clue? Have you discussed it at all?

GEORGIE. Not really. I never really found a good opening.

WALLY. You said she was crazy about you.

GEORGIE. I think she is. She does little things that tell me she loves me. Like her body language, for instance. Whenever we're alone, her face gets all flushed and she becomes breathless. I read that if a woman gets flushed and breathless that means she has romantic feelings.

WALLY. Either that or she has asthma.

GEORGIE. And she plays with her hair whenever she talks to me. I read somewhere that if a woman plays with her hair, she's attracted to you.

WALLY. Maybe she has bugs. You ever think of that? I thought this was going to be a tryst with the love of your life. Instead I set up a meeting with you and a wheezing woman with head lice?

GEORGIE. Hey, watch what you say.

WALLY. This is hopeless. When's the last time you seduced a woman?

GEORGIE. I can't remember. I don't think I've ever seduced a woman in my life.

WALLY. What about Arlene?

GEORGIE. I never seduced her. She just yelled at me until I took my pants off.

WALLY. Look, you want to cut some corners here and show Heather exactly how you feel?

GEORGIE. Yes.

WALLY. Take off your clothes.

GEORGIE. Why? I don't trust you.

WALLY. The only thing those clothes inspire any woman to do is her taxes.

GEORGIE. I didn't bring anything else.

WALLY. (*Heading for dresser.*) I did.

GEORGIE. What? I'm not wearing anything weird.

(*WALLY takes silk pajamas from dresser.*)

WALLY. Put these silk pajamas on. These are romantic.

GEORGIE. (*Strips to boxers and a t-shirt.*) They're great.

WALLY. I stole them out of a room downstairs. These are very sexy. You'll drive her wild with desire.

GEORGIE. I will?

WALLY. I was gonna save them for myself, but you're in worse shape than I am.

GEORGIE. Get out. She'll be here any minute.

WALLY. I'm going. I'm going. Give me your clothes.

(*GEORGIE hands him his clothes. WALLY still holds onto the pajamas.*)

GEORGIE. Here. Hey, you better let me have the pajamas.

WALLY. (*Keeps the pajamas out of Georgie's reach.*) Georgie. Think of this as an ice-breaker.

I'm doing this for your own good. You'll thank me later.

GEORGIE. Hey!

WALLY. Have fun, Love God.

(WALLY exits with the suitcase, Georgie's clothes and the pajamas.)

GEORGIE. That's not funny,Wally. Wally! Wally? Oh, Wally?!

(There is a RATTLE at the door. GEORGIE panics. HE runs in circles. HE pulls his T-shirt down to cover his knees and walks to the door.)

GEORGIE. Heather?

A MAN'S VOICE. *(Off.)* What?

GEORGIE. Oh, God. Mr. President?

MAN. *(Off.)* What?

GEORGIE. Uh . . . Who's there?

MR. BICKHARDT. *(Off.)* Hotel Manager.

GEORGIE. Oh, God.

(GEORGIE opens the door. An imposing hotel manager, MR.BICKHARDT, enters.)

GEORGIE. I can explain.

MR. BICKHARDT. Did anyone see you come in?

GEORGIE. Absolutely not. No one saw me. This was my own idea. I'm terribly sorry about all of this. It'll never happen again. If I can just find my pants . . .

MR. BICKHARDT. It's our pleasure.

GEORGIE. How's that?

MR. BICKHARDT. I said it's our pleasure to have you here.

GEORGIE. It is? Then . . . you know why I'm here?

MR. BICKHARDT. I would think so. I *am* the hotel manager. Terrence Bickhardt. (*Shakes his hand.*)

GEORGIE. (*Tentatively.*) How do you do?

MR. BICKHARDT. This is an exciting weekend for all of us.

GEORGIE. Oh, God. Who else did he tell?

MR. BICKHARDT. The entire security staff.

GEORGIE. The whole staff?

MR. BICKHARDT. We'll all be watching you.

GEORGIE. Watching me? I don't want anyone watching me.

MR. BICKHARDT. But, Mr. . . .

GEORGIE. I don't want anyone coming in here!

MR. BICKHARDT. Very well. All right, all right. Now, don't be nervous.

GEORGIE. I can't help it. I don't do this every day.

MR. BICKHARDT. I should hope not. You might have been dead a long time ago.

GEORGIE. I am a bit of a tiger.

MR. BICKHARDT. If you don't mind my asking . . . where's your protection?

GEORGIE. Oh. In . . . my pants pocket.

MR. BICKHARDT. Packing heat?

GEORGIE. I don't remember the brand name.

MR. BICKHARDT. You really shouldn't be alone here. Considering.

GEORGIE. Oh, she'll be here soon.

MR. BICKHARDT. "She?" I thought you'd be with a man.

GEORGIE. Why?

MR. BICKHARDT. I just assumed you'd like it better.

GEORGIE. Oh, really?

MR. BICKHARDT. Call me old-fashioned. I'll send you up a man.

GEORGIE. I don't want a man! I've got a girl coming.

MR. BICKHARDT. Very well, Mr. Fish. Have it your way. While you're waiting, may I send you up something from our kitchen?

GEORGIE. "Fish?"

MR. BICKHARDT. Very good. We have a lovely grilled salmon today.

GEORGIE. What?

MR. BICKHARDT. Just relax. You're in safe hands here, Mr. Fish.

GEORGIE. Uh . . . I am? Uh . . . thank you.

MR. BICKHARDT. Keep the shades drawn
and leave everything to us.
GEORGIE. I'll do that.

(*MR. BICKHARDT exits. GEORGIE is
    confused.*)

GEORGIE. Who's Mr. Fish?

(*The door bursts open, pinning GEORGIE behind
    the US door. A man in dark sunglasses
    (STAN KEMRITE, CIA Agent) bursts into the
    room, gun drawn.*)

STAN. (*Calling to hallway.*) Stay back, Mr.
Fish. I'll check the room out.

(*STAN KEMRITE moves through the room
    checking it out in exaggerated "CIA" secret
    service-like moves. When Georgie has an
    opening HE dives under the bed. STAN
    checks out the closet, the bathroom, and then
    crosses between the bed and the bathroom. As
    HE bends down to check out under the bed,
    GEORGIE pops out the other side and runs
    over the bed, exiting into the bathroom as
    STAN pops out from under the bed SR and then
    crosses between the bed and the bathroom. As
    HE bends down to check out under the bed,
    GEORGIE pops out the other side and runs*)

over the bed, exiting into the bathroom as STAN pops out from under the bed SR.)

STAN. All clear! Come in, Mr.Fish.

(ROGER FISH enters. HE is a mild-mannered writer of fiction. HE carries a book.)

ROGER. Are you sure I'm safe here?

STAN. Those terrorist vermin will never find you.

ROGER. All this for a book.

STAN. A damn good book if you don't mind my saying.

ROGER. Thank you. You know what the odds of someone killing me for writing a book are? It would be like *(Gropes for an analogy.)* If I took . . . all these pens, *(Takes seven pens from his breast pocket.)* flipped them into the air . . . and all seven stuck in the ceiling . . . spelling out the word "albino." That's how rare this is.

STAN. I don't think it's that rare. Of course, I haven't read your book. But calling the Obodanza of La Banza a big fat pig. All of America's behind you.

ROGER. I didn't call the Obodanza of La Banza a big fat pig. All I said was that he used a large ham radio.

STAN. Good story. Stick with it.

ROGER. When do I see my daughter?

STAN. She's hidden away. At an undisclosed area. Tomorrow we'll move you and your daughter to a "safe house" in Wyoming.

ROGER. What's this on the bed?

STAN. Stand back. It might be a trap.

(*STAN throws Roger out of the way. HE flies into the DSR chair. STAN pulverizes the flowers and candy. Then tosses them out the window.*)

STAN. Might have been a bomb.

ROGER. Was it a bomb?

STAN. No. It was a bunch of crushed flowers and smashed candy.

ROGER. Why did you throw them out the window?

STAN. Agency procedure.

ROGER. Why was it in the room?

STAN. The hotel probably wanted to welcome you. You're a big celebrity in this town.

ROGER. They know I'm here?

STAN. Just the security staff. And they know you're not to be disturbed.

ROGER. Then who sent them up here?

STAN. A careless bellboy no doubt.

(*The door begins to open.*)

STAN. Stand back!

(HE pushes Roger backwards. HE falls over the bed. ROGER screams. STAN turns to shoot him, catches himself and points the gun at the maid, MISSY, who enters.)

MISSY. Don't shoot! Just use the "Do Not Disturb" sign!

STAN. Sorry. *(To Roger.)* Are you all right?

ROGER. I fell on my pencil. *(Pulls pencil out of his backside.)*

STAN. Who are you?

MISSY. Missy. Who are you?

STAN. This room is empty.

MISSY. What are you, a mirage?

STAN. We're not here. Get it?

MISSY. *(To Roger.)* What is he saying?

ROGER. He's saying please pretend we're not here. We're hiding out.

STAN. Hey, Mr. Bigmouth. You want to leave everything to me?

MISSY. You're hiding out? Really?

STAN. Not us! We're guarding someone.

MISSY. Who? Robert Goulet?

ROGER. What?

STAN. We'd rather not say.

MISSY. I won't tell anyone.

STAN. Please, Miss. Stan Kemrite *(Flashing badge.)* CIA. You have seen nothing. You know nothing. You will say nothing. Agreed? Agreed? Say something.

MISSY. You just told me to say nothing.

ROGER. If anyone knows we're here, it could cost a man his life.

MISSY. Who?

STAN. We can't say.

MISSY. Where is he?

STAN. (*Indicates bathroom.*) In there.

MISSY. Can I guess who it is?

STAN. No.

MISSY. Is it Perry Como?

STAN. No.

(*WALLY enters pushing a serving cart with a fish dinner on it.*)

WALLY. Here's your Grilled Salmon Almondine, Love Machine.

ROGER. Thank you.

MISSY. Hi, Wally.

(*STAN throws Wally against a wall and frisks him.*)

STAN. Spread'em, bellboy.

WALLY. I guess a tip is out of the question. Who the hell are you guys?

ROGER. (*To Missy.*) You know this man?

MISSY. Yes, it's Wally. My boyfriend. He's okay. He works here!

(*STAN lets up on Wally.*)

WALLY. The manager said to send this up. Watch the hands, sailor. I thought my brother ordered it.

STAN. Do I look like your brother?

WALLY. No. But you walk like my Aunt Helen.

STAN. Why you . . .

ROGER. I didn't order anything to eat.

STAN. Stand back. It might be a trap. (*Proceeds to mush HIS hands through the food, checking for a bomb.*)

WALLY. Hey, don't play with your food.

STAN. Shut up, you.

WALLY. (*To Missy.*) What are you doing in here?

MISSY. I was gonna rehearse a monologue for my acting class. (*To Stan and Roger.*) I'm an actress.

STAN. All clear. No bomb here.

ROGER. I really think you have the wrong room, Bellboy.

WALLY. Sorry. I'll try next door. (*Looks desperately for his brother as HE wheels the food out. HE sticks his hand out for a tip, as an excuse to look for Georgie longer.*)

STAN. Get lost, Curious George.

(*WALLY exits. MISSY sees the book.*)

MISSY. Where'd you get this book? You have to cross picket lines for this.

ROGER. You know about this book?

MISSY. Hey, that's who you're guarding isn't it?

STAN. Um . . . I'm not saying it is. And I'm not saying it isn't.

MISSY. It is.

ROGER. You're a master of secrecy.

MISSY. I think it's terrible what's happened. Poor guy writes a dumb book and the next thing you know half the world is fighting over his right to write it.

STAN. There's only one book I care about, lady. (*Pulls out CIA manual.*) The CIA handbook. (*HE drops the book.*)

MISSY. Thanks. Call me Missy. Maybe you've heard of me. Missy Ffrench? With two "fs"?

STAN. Sorry.

MISSY. You will someday. I'm not gonna be a maid all my life. I have a plan. The only girls who get any attention nowadays are the ones who sleep with evangelists and ballplayers. Someone who makes news. Like the author of your book for instance. So, I figure if I sleep with someone like him, I could sell the story to Playboy and get a couple TV-movie deals, go on Donahue and Oprah, and probably get a jean commercial.

STAN. And that's why you're a maid?

MISSY. What better place to meet celebrities in bed than New York's finest hotel?

STAN. Good plan.

ROGER. What are you saying? That's a terrible plan! What about hard work, talent and perseverance?

MISSY. It takes too long. I'm almost 23, you know. Life is short.

ROGER. What about your boyfriend?

MISSY. He doesn't want to be an actress. Hey, what about (*Referring to offstage person.*) him? Do you think he'd be interested?

STAN. Who? (*Realizing.*) Oh, him? I don't think so. He's . . . a very private guy.

ROGER. Not so fast. He might be interested.

MISSY. Oh, good.

STAN. No he wouldn't be interested! Not at all!

ROGER. Well . . . we could ask him.

MISSY. Great. Imagine the publicity!

ROGER. Tell me what you thought of the book.

MISSY. Oh, I haven't read it. I'm waiting for the *People Magazine* excerpts.

STAN. You'd better get out. We could lose our jobs.

MISSY. Hey, if Mr. Fish is interested, let me know, okay? (*SHE exits.*)

ROGER. Boy, she's cute.

STAN. Mr. Fish. You want to risk your life for seven minutes of fun?

ROGER. Seven?

STAN. I was including drinks.

ROGER. Of course not.

STAN. All right, then.

ROGER. Do you mind if I take a shower? You people've moved me from van to van to car to hotel. I'm exhausted and grungy.

STAN. Shower? Let me check it out.

(*STAN whips out his pistol. It flies across the room. It FIRES. STAN and ROGER jump.*)

STAN. Stand back!

(*STAN pushes Roger backwards and HE falls over a chair.*)

STAN. Stay here. Get off the floor!

ROGER. I'm doomed!

STAN. Trust me, Mr. Fish. I was number six in my class. I'm very good.

ROGER. How many were in your class?

STAN. Seven. But Number Five was a cheater. He copied off of Number Two.

(*Outside the window, WALLY sneaks by from SR. HE stops at the USR window to look for Georgie. Then exits SR.*)

ROGER. I'm taking a shower.

STAN. (*Picking up pistol.*) Okay. Let's go.

ROGER. I usually shower alone.

STAN. Not anymore. How do I know you're not the suicidal type?

ROGER. If I were suicidal I'd let the terrorists kill me.

STAN. Exactly. As long as Stan Kemrite is on the case, I'll be sticking to you like a fat lady's panties.

(*THEY exit to the shower. GEORGIE enters from the window ledge SL. HE is panicked. WALLY sneaks in the the SR door as GEORGIE climbs in the SL window. WALLY taps him on the shoulder. GEORGIE jumps in fear.*)

GEORGIE. Ah!

(*HE in turn scares WALLY, who screams. THEY cover each other's mouths.*)

GEORGIE. What's the matter with you?

WALLY. Where have you been?

GEORGIE. Feeding the pigeons, where do you think I've been? You said no one would be using this room! Who are these people?

WALLY. I have no idea. But they have a violent reaction to grilled salmon.

GEORGIE. Get me my pants!

WALLY. All right. Don't panic. I'll be right back. Stay here. And don't let them find you.

GEORGIE. Where am I going to go?

(*WALLY exits out the door.*
SFX: SHOWER STARTS.
GEORGIE goes to telephone and dials.)

GEORGIE. Hello? Operator. Can you tell me
who's in Room 2725? . . . Yes, I know I'm calling
from 2725 . . . I have amnesia. I . . . Hello?

(*HE hangs up as MISSY re-enters from the hall.*
HE turns to see her and screams, which scares
her.)

MISSY. Hello. We haven't met.
GEORGIE. God you scared the pants off me.
Oh. (*Covers himself with a pillow.*) I mean, who
are you?

MISSY. Missy Ffrench. With two "fs." Ever
heard of me?
GEORGIE. No.
MISSY. You will someday. Are you him?
GEORGIE. Him?
MISSY. You were just in the bathroom,
weren't you?
GEORGIE. Well, yes.
MISSY. (*Refers to novel.*) I'm a big fan of
yours.
GEORGIE. You've seen me in the bathroom
before?
MISSY. Where'd those two guys go?

GEORGIE. They're in the shower. But they won't be long.

MISSY. Did they tell you my plan?

GEORGIE. Huh? Oh, . . . sure.

MISSY. What do you think?

GEORGIE. Oh . . . it sounds great. Look, when they're done in there, you gotta be gone!

MISSY. You mean it?

GEORGIE. Yes, I mean it!

MISSY. Wow. This was easier than I thought. (*SHE begins removing her uniform.*)

GEORGIE. What are you doing?

MISSY. You said you were in a hurry.

GEORGIE. Are you crazy? Put that . . .

MISSY. The water's still running. (*Lays down on the bed.*) Hurry up. I still have to bring towels to Room 410.

GEORGIE. What? Get up from there.

(*There is a KNOCK at the door.*)

HEATHER. (*Off.*) Mr. Leach!

GEORGIE. Heather!

MISSY. Who's that?

GEORGIE. My . . . girl . . . my secre . . . my daughter. (*To door.*) I'll be right there, little one.

MISSY. (*Getting her dress.*) Why did your daughter call you, "Mr. Leach?"

GEORGIE. Uh . . .

MISSY. Is it code?

GEORGIE. A little bit. But you'd be too if you didn't have pants on.

MISSY. Is "Leach" code for "Fish?"

GEORGIE. Lady, I don't know what the hell you're talking about.

MISSY. Don't worry about me. "Mum's" the word.

GEORGIE. (*To Missy.*) Okay, Mum, get the hell out of here.

HEATHER. (*Off.*) What?

GEORGIE. Nothing kitten. (*To Missy.*) Go. Please. She's just a little girl.

MISSY. I'll be back later.

(*SFX: SHOWER STOPS.*
MISSY heads for the door.)

GEORGIE. No! You can't go out that way! I have no pants on!

MISSY. Well . . . Where should I go?

GEORGIE. Over . . . in the . . . Out on the ledge!

MISSY. We're twenty-seven stories up. I could slip off!

GEORGIE. The cars will break your fall! (*Running back and forth between the bathroom and the front door.*) Please! They're toweling off in there by now!

MISSY. I have a passkey. I'll go next door. Maybe it's someone famous.

GEORGIE. Good. Go!

MISSY. (*Goes to adjoining room door SL and unlocks it.*) Anyone in here? (*Looking off.*) What a slob! (*Exits next door.*)

HEATHER. (*Off.*) Is everything all right?

GEORGIE. (*Hides under the sheet.*) Come in.

(*We hear HEATHER walk face first into the door.*)

HEATHER. (*Off.*) It's locked!

GEORGIE. Oh!

(*HE rises and answers the door – pantless. HEATHER, the secretary, enters. SHE is all business and a bit repressed.*)

HEATHER. Mr. Leach. Your pants.

GEORGIE. This isn't what it looks like.

HEATHER. It looks like you have no pants on.

GEORGIE. Well, I guess that part looks right. This isn't . . . there's a reason I'm . . .

HEATHER. (*Scratches her head. Uncomfortable, but flattered.*) Mr. Leach . . . I thought you asked me here for business.

GEORGIE. I did. I mean . . . I said that. I mean . . . Heather, there's something I've wanted to tell you for a long time.

HEATHER. Am I fired?

GEORGIE. No.

HEATHER. I know there's a problem with the books. But I've been working nights and weekends trying to find that missing decimal point. I don't know why you've kept me on so long.

GEORGIE. I'm not firing you.

HEATHER. Oh, I'm glad. I never was any good with computers. There's too many things to press.

GEORGIE. Heather . . . I asked you here because . . . I've wanted to confess something to you ever since the first day you sat across from my credenza.

(*SFX: SHOWER STARTS.*)

    HEATHER. (*Hearing shower.*) What's that?
    GEORGIE. It's like a desk.
    HEATHER. No. That noise.
    GEORGIE. Oh, it's nothing.
    HEATHER. Who's in there?
    GEORGIE. Who's in there?
    HEATHER. Who is that?

GEORGIE. I . . . uh . . . I got an unexpected visit from my . . . brother, you see. He has a problem and came to me for advice.

(*Offstage ROGER sings: "Moon River."*)

    HEATHER. (*Rising.*) Is that your brother?
    GEORGIE. Yes. It is.

(*Offstage ROGER and STAN harmonize.*)

HEATHER. What's that?

GEORGIE. That's his problem. He's always bringing strange men around and . . . showering with them . . . wherever I go.

HEATHER. Oh. Maybe I should leave.

GEORGIE. No, please don't go. Why don't you wait . . . down in the bar. I'll get rid of my brother and his soapy little friend, and I'll meet you.

(*SFX: SHOWER STOPS.*)

HEATHER. Wait alone in a New York bar? Mr. Leach . . . I could be propositioned or even molested.

GEORGIE. It would mean so much to me. (*Reacts.*) If you waited, I mean.

HEATHER. Well . . . you know I'd do anything for you. (*Plays with her hair.*) I've wanted to say that for so long.

(*Offstage NOISE of STAN and ROGER.*)

GEORGIE. (*Shoving her out.*) So long.

(*GEORGIE slams the door in her face. STAN enters from the bathroom, in his pants and T-shirt, with wet hair and a towel around his neck as GEORGIE hides under the bed. STAN checks the room out.*)

STAN. All clear!

(*STAN wipes his hair dry as ROGER enters in his pants and T-shirt, wiping his hair with a towel.*)

ROGER. I don't think I like this conditioner.

STAN. Really? It smells so nice and fresh.

WALLY. (*Enters out of breath, carrying pants.*) Here are the pants you ordered . . . Yipes. I mean . . . (*HE realizes HE is once again talking to Stan and Roger.*)

ROGER. (*Takes pants.*) Thanks.

STAN. What is your problem?

WALLY. (*Confused.*) Me? Cheapskates who tip badly. What's your problem?

STAN. Will you get out!

WALLY. Will you be taking a shower again soon?

STAN. No!

WALLY. Too bad. That conditioner smells awful.

STAN. Out!

(*WALLY exits.*)

STAN. This hotel's going to hell.

ROGER. Did you see what I did with my other shoe?

(*From under the R side of the bed, GEORGIE tosses Roger's shoe into his waiting hands.*)

ROGER. (*To Stan.*) Thanks.

STAN. For what?

ROGER. For nothing. Hey, wait a minute. I didn't order any pants pressed.

STAN. Stand back. It might be a trick.

(*ROGER hits the ground. STAN kneels on the bed and shreds the pants with a knife.*)

STAN. All clear.

ROGER. (*Rising.*) Thanks. That was close. Was there a bomb in there?

STAN. No, just a lot of cheap fabric.

ROGER. I couldn't have gotten killed?

STAN. No, but you might've gotten a nasty rash.

ROGER. I hate living like this! It's like I'm a human dartboard . . . and I'm getting hit with darts but one of the darts is poisonous, except I don't know which one it is. Know what I mean?

STAN. I don't think so.

ROGER. I can't trust anyone!

STAN. Is that what you said? Mr. Fish. Just relax. Two days of hiding out and you'll be safely on your way to Wyoming.

ROGER. Where is my daughter?

STAN. I can't tell you where she is. Agency procedure.

ROGER. She's twelve years old! She's probably scared to death. I bet she's as scared as if . . . (*HE looks around for an analogy.*) you started running on the roof of that building over there real fast and then leapt across to this building and half way here you realized the window was closed . . . *That's* how scared she is.

STAN. She's perfectly safe. We have a crack agent guarding her. Number five in his class.

ROGER. Number five? The cheater?

STAN. Calm down, Mr. Fish.

ROGER. Tell me where she is.

STAN. I can't. Someone in the hotel may see you and then your cover will be blown wide open.

ROGER. She's in the hotel?

STAN. I didn't say that.

ROGER. Can't she just come down and stay with me?

STAN. There are death threats against you. What happens if I screw up and you get killed? She could be caught in the line of fire.

ROGER. I guess you're right. What do you mean if you screw up??

(*STAN shrugs and drops his gun.*)

STAN. Sorry about that. It sort of slipped. I shouldn't have used that moisturizing hand lotion.

ROGER. Yes, but it makes your hands so nice and smooth. I'm gonna go see her. What room was it again?

STAN. 1648. I mean . . .

ROGER. Thanks. 1648.

(*ROGER heads for the door. STAN blocks his way.*)

STAN. You can't. You'll lose your life. I'll lose my job.

ROGER. You can either come with me or stay behind.

STAN. You can't leave this room, Mr. Fish. The handbook clearly states (*Reads from manual.*) I'll have to shoot you dead.

ROGER. Doesn't that defeat the purpose of you guarding me?

STAN. Well, yes. I guess it does. (*Thinks.*) So, I guess . . . now I'm confused.

ROGER. There must be some way to see her.

STAN. Well, I guess if you were disguised somehow.

ROGER. But how?

WALLY. (*Enters, breathless and frantic.*) Your wife is in the lobby! (*HE sees Stan and Roger.*)

STAN. I don't have a wife.

ROGER. My wife died.

WALLY. Oh . . . then it must have been someone else's wife. I'll stall her.

STAN. Get out of here!

(*WALLY exits.*)

STAN. Was that the same bellhop who came in here before?

ROGER. I guess so. I didn't catch his face.

STAN. Me neither. I know it's rude, but I never really look at the faces of . . .

(*ROGER and STAN react.*)

ROGER & STAN. Bellhops!

STAN. There's a storage closet down the hall. Two bellhop uniforms coming up.

ROGER. Thank you.

STAN. Just for an hour. Then right back here.

ROGER. I promise.

STAN. Let's go. (*Checks out hotel door.*) All clear. Hustle. Hustle.

ROGER. You know what this feels like? Like if I were in the desert and saw a mirage and right as I crawled to it, parched, lips cracking, dehydrated, it rained on me.

STAN. Will you come on!

(*THEY exit. GEORGIE crawls out.*)

GEORGIE. They have guns! They could shoot the fruit right off my loom! (*Sees pants on the bed.*) Great! Pants!

(*GEORGIE tries slipping on the shredded pants. There is nothing left for him to put a leg into, despite trying three or four sttempts. WALLY bursts in.*)

WALLY. Room service. Did you order . . . Hey . . . Which way did they go, Georgie?

GEORGIE. They just left! Who are they? They have guns!

WALLY. Good, cause you need one. She's coming this way! Stop dancing. I'm talking to you! Arlene's on her way up! I'm sorry, Georgie. I tried stalling her. I really did.

GEORGIE. How did you do that?

WALLY. Well, first I tripped her in the lobby. Then I jammed the elevators, so she'd have to walk up twenty-seven flights of stairs, and then I paid a maid to butt her a few times with her housecleaning cart.

GEORGIE. Gee, thanks Wally. You're all heart.

(*MISSY enters from the adjoining room. The MAN in the next room BELLOWS.*)

GUEST. And stay out!! (*Exits into his room, SLAMMING the door.*)

MISSY. Sorry! The grouch next door is back. And he's a nobody. Is she gone?

WALLY. No, she's coming.

MISSY. Hi, Wally.

WALLY. Hi, Missy.

MISSY. Who's coming?

WALLY. Who's gone?

MISSY. His daughter.

WALLY. Your what?

GEORGIE. My daughter! (*To Missy.*) Yes. She's gone. But she'll be back. And a bigger one's on her way.

WALLY. What are you doing with my brother?

MISSY. Mr. Fish is your brother? You never told me that.

WALLY. Who?

GEORGIE. Me.

MISSY. (*Sotto.*) Fish is Leach.

WALLY. What?

MISSY. Code. It's a code.

WALLY. Well, I hope it clears up, it's affecting your voice.

(*A POUNDING on the door.*)

ARLENE. (*Off.*) Open it, or I'll knock it down!

MISSY. Oh, no. They found you!

GEORGIE. (*To Wally.*) Is that . . . ?

WALLY. The Amityville Horror! Hide quick.

(*GEORGIE and WALLY run in opposite directions, knocking each other down.*)

MISSY. Call security.
GEORGIE & WALLY. No!
WALLY. If we call security they'll know we're in here!
MISSY. But you're in danger!
GEORGIE. I don't care!
MISSY. If they kill you, will you try to die in my arms?
GEORGIE. I'll do my best.
MISSY. Thanks!
GUEST. (*The GUEST from the next room steps out.*) Will you people shut up!! (*HE SLAMS his door shut.*)
WALLY. Quick! The adjoining room.

(*The THREESOME run into the locked door.*)

MISSY. Oh, my chin!
GEORGIE. Oh, my nose!

(*ARLENE pounds on the door.*)

WALLY. Omigod!
GEORGIE. The bathroom, Missy. (*Re: Arlene.*) Get rid of her, Wally.

WALLY. Me?

(*MISSY and GEORGIE exit to the bathroom. WALLY goes to door, crosses himself and timidly opens the door. ARLENE enters. SHE is grotesque, loud, fat and crass. SHE wears black pants, has black hair and a mustache. SHE sizes the room up and begins searching around.*)

ARLENE. Where in the hell is he? I'll rip his lungs out!
WALLY. Oh, hi Arlene. What brings you here? A crane?
ARLENE. (*Sizing him up.*) Oh, look at this. If vomit could wear shoes . . .
WALLY. Something wrong, Arlene? All the color's drained out of the varicose veins in your face.
ARLENE. Get out of my way, Wally, or I'll make your chin even longer than it is.
WALLY. There's no one here.
ARLENE. (*Looks in the closet.*) I know he's here. He left a note with the hotel name and this room number on it.
WALLY. He left a note?

(*Behind them MISSY walks past on the ledge L to R as ARLENE peeks under the bed.*)

ARLENE. I'm gonna find him and I'm gonna rip his intestines out through his mouth.

WALLY. With those stubby little arms?

ARLENE. Where is he? (*Ransacks the bureau drawers.*)

WALLY. He hasn't hidden in a bureau since he was two-foot, three.

ARLENE. Shut up, Baggage-Boy, or two-foot, three's gonna look real tall to you.

WALLY. He's in the shower.

ARLENE. I don't hear any shower.

(*SFX: SHOWER starts.*)

ARLENE. (*Goes to bathroom door and POUNDS.*) Open the door, George. I know you're in there.

(*WALLY gets an idea and exits out the window, walking on the ledge towards the bathroom SL. ARLENE never sees him leave.*)

ARLENE. You don't think I know what's going on, but I'm wise to you, Ratboy. You think I'll divorce you now? I'll suck you dry of every cent you make and every breath you take. I'll cripple you. I'll make your life so miserable you'll have to get botulism just to have a good time. (*SHE POUNDS some more.*) I'm gonna give you until three. Then I'm coming in! One. Two.

(*The bathroom door opens and GEORGE is pushed out from behind. HE wears an ill-fitting bellhop uniform and hat.*)

GEORGIE. (*Innocent.*) Oh, hi Arlene. What brings you here?

ARLENE. What are you doing?

GEORGIE. What do you mean?

ARLENE. Why are you wearing that stupid uniform?

GEORGIE. Oh, this uniform?

ARLENE. Yes.

GEORGIE. I . . . uh . . . I work here.

ARLENE. Work here?

GEORGIE. At this hotel. I'm a bellboy.

ARLENE. Since when?

GEORGIE. Since . . . tonight.

ARLENE. You're a successful accountant. Why would you want to work as a bellboy?

GEORGIE. Well, dear, you know I haven't been pulling in any new accounts. In fact I've been losing accounts since you started visiting me at the office.

ARLENE. What about it?

GEORGIE. So, I thought I'd come to work here with Wally. Pick up a little extra money for those lyposuction operations you want so bad.

ARLENE. Is that so? Then why are you in this room?

GEORGIE. This is . . . the bellhop lounge. One room per floor. We change in here, relax between luggage runs . . .

ARLENE. Oh, really? And I suppose Wally will . . . (*Notices he's gone.*) Where's Wally?

(*Behind them, on the ledge, WALLY – in boxers and T-shirt, scurries along. SL to SR. HE exits out of sight.*)

GEORGIE. He's working.

ARLENE. And where are all the other bellhops?

GEORGIE. Out . . . belling and hopping.

ARLENE. Well, then get back to work. You lazy slob. You want to lose this job?

GEORGIE. No, Arlene.

ARLENE. Then get out.

GEORGIE. And what will you be doing?

ARLENE. "Lounging" right here. And you can deposit your tips with me.

GEORGIE. Swell. (*Exits.*)

ARLENE. How stupid do you think I am, you shrivelled little excuse of a man?

(*SHE rummages through the room looking for something, as behind her from the window ledge, enters a menacing man in a long black coat, black boots and black turtleneck, with a mustache, long hair and an earring. HE carries a pack, which HE deposits by the window.)*

BABU. You shall die, vermin pig dog!

ARLENE. Get a load of you. What are you, a musician?

BABU. I know he is here. You cannot hide the lamb. I shall cut out his heart. You wear the colors. Are you one of us?

ARLENE. I'm Polish. Who the hell are you? You look like a clown.

BABU. I am not a clown.

ARLENE. How'd you know he was here?

BABU. I have my ways.

ARLENE. I found a note. You're the girl's husband?

BABU. Who?

ARLENE. You don't think I fell for the cockamamie bellboy story, do you?

BABU. No I would not think so.

ARLENE. He's running around the hotel in his little uniform, but he's not fooling anyone.

BABU. I shall kill him. It shall be I.

ARLENE. You gotta work on that English. What are you, Puerto Rican?

BABU. The dog shall die.

ARLENE. Get in line, Pedro.

BABU. Babu Rashaad.

ARLENE. Well, sit down and maybe it'll go away. I'm going down to check out the bar. If you

find them first, don't kill them until I get back. I
want to watch the expression of pain on his face.

(*ARLENE exits to lobby. BABU sees the well-
stocked bar and plush surroundings.*)

BABU. Capitalist pigs. Full room of drinks.
While others die from thirst. Food that can feed
hundreds rotting. (*Sniffs.*) Cod, if I'm not
mistaken. This book is proof of his vile existence.
I will avenge the blasphemy. I, Babu, will commit
the perfect act of revenge. Kill the man who goes
by the name of Fish. Stab him through the heart to
release his evil spirit and over his face I shall
place the Mask of the Pig. (*Pulls out a rubber pig
mask.*) He shall die quickly, quietly. Killed by
the gods, wearing the Mask of the Pig to show his
guilt. At last I shall have my revenge! The bellhop
shall die the death of a dog!

(*BABU makes wild DESERT NOISES as HE
attacks the novel with a knife. Keys
JINGLING at the door scare him into hiding
in the closet DSR. STAN and ROGER enter,
dressed as bellhops – laden down with
luggage.*)

ROGER. Where the hell is she, Kemrite?
STAN. I don't know. They must have moved
her to another floor for security reasons.

ROGER. Call your men! I want to know where the hell she is right now!

STAN. I can't do that. Besides, we have to bring these bags down to Room 523.

ROGER. Let me explain something to you. Every time you tell me I can't see my daughter, it's like . . . (*Looks around.*) a matador waving a red flag in front of a bull and then telling the bull, "Don't move, Bull, you're in a china shop!

STAN. I can't contact anyone! Our policy is if I don't have the information they want the terrorists will get nothing out of us when they torture us!

ROGER. So instead they'll just torture us . . . indefinitely.

STAN. Uh . . . Yes. According to the manual.

ROGER. We are searching every room on every floor of this hotel until we find her. Are you coming?

STAN. Well . . . okay. As long as we can pool our tips.

(*THEY exit SR with the suitcases. BABU enters from the closet. HE hears a NOISE at the door and hides back inside the closet. HEATHER enters the SR door.*)

HEATHER. Mr. Leach? Hello? (*Scanning room.*) A man grabbed my knee. Hello?

(*HEATHER exits to the bathroom searching for Georgie. BABU peeks out from the closet with his dagger drawn. GEORGIE enters SR, still dressed in his bellboy uniform. BABU closes the closet door.*)

GEORGIE. Where did she go? Heather, are you in here?

(*GEORGIE passes the closet. BABU opens the door. Before he can step out, HEATHER reenters from the bathroom. The closet door reshuts.*)

HEATHER. Mr. Leach?
GEORGIE. What are you doing in here?
HEATHER. A man grabbed my knee in the bar.
GEORGIE. We have to get out of here.
HEATHER. Whatever it is, I can face it with you.
GEORGIE. No, you can't. It's worse than you can possibly know.
HEATHER. What are you wearing?
GEORGIE. I'm hiding.
HEATHER. Why?
GEORGIE. Please, we have to leave here. I'm in way over my head.
HEATHER. Oh, Mr. Leach. Now it all makes sense.
GEORGIE. What does?

HEATHER. I know the accounts at the office have been short, but I never suspected you! I thought it was my Macintosh.

GEORGIE. What are you talking about?

HEATHER. That's why you asked me here, isn't it? To confess! You embezzled $500,000 from Bendetson, Bendetson & Howard!

GEORGIE. What?

HEATHER. (*Playing with her hair.*) I'll stand by you.

GEORGIE. $500,000? That's the missing decimal point you were talking about? $500,000? Why didn't you say something earlier?!

HEATHER. I didn't suspect you!

GEORGIE. I have no idea what you're talking about.

HEATHER. Stick with that story. I won't give you away.

GEORGIE. Give me away? To who?

HEATHER. The Feds.

GEORGIE. The Feds?

(*Someone begins to open the door.*)

GEORGIE. Oh, God. Listen to me. They think I'm Mr. Fish but . . .

HEATHER. Oh, Mr. Leach.

GEORGIE. You can't call me Mr. Leach. Don't you understand? I'm Mr. Fish! You have to call me Mr. Fish!

HEATHER. I'll never call you anything but!

(BABU reacts to "Mr. Fish." HE hides again as WALLY enters with a cart of party favors – balloons, helium cannister, etc.)

GEORGIE. Oh, it's you.

WALLY. *(To Heather.)* Hi, how are you? *(To Georgie.)* Someone knows you're here and is on their way back up.

HEATHER. Oh no!

GEORGIE. I thought I lost that person in the lounge. Heather, how would you like to take a bath?

HEATHER. No, thank you. I should stay here, in case you need me.

GEORGIE. Gee, that's sweet of you. *(Pours a glass of water and throws it on her shirt.)* Whoops. Gee, it must've slipped.

HEATHER. Oh, I better go wash this off before it sets.

GEORGIE. Great idea.

(HEATHER exits to bathroom.)

GEORGIE. What's going on?

WALLY. Your fat-pig wife was guzzling Stoli-stingers in the bar! And you know how mean she gets when she drinks! She had grown men sobbing just describing what she was gonna do to you.

GEORGIE. Oh God, what will I do?

WALLY. Don't worry. I sent Missy up to tell security that a suspicious-looking person was in the lounge.

GEORGIE. Arlene?

WALLY. It might just slow her up long enough to get you out of here. Gotta run. Big party in the Walter Raleigh Room. I get to blow up two hundred helium balloons.

GEORGIE. Have fun. I'm getting out of here. Hurry up, Heather!

(WALLY opens the door and MR. BICKHARDT enters.)

MR. BICKHARDT. Mr. Fish!

WALLY. Who? Mr. Bickhardt, do you have a cold too?

MR. BICKHARDT. Certainly not. What are you doing in here, Mr. Leach?

GEORGIE. Well . . . to tell the truth . . .

MR. BICKHARDT. Don't stick up for him, Mr. Fish. This room is off limits.

GEORGIE. Huh?

WALLY. Mr. Fish? Author of "The Satanic Nurses?" That's who's in this room? I mean *(To Georgie.)* you're *that* Mr. Fish?

GEORGIE. That's me.

(BABU's head pops out.)

MR. BICKHARDT. I'm afraid I have some bad news. A suspicious looking character was spotted in the lounge. You're safest staying right here in this room. Where's your girl?

GEORGIE. Washing her bullets.

MR. BICKHARDT. There is a guard posted on each floor. The CIA has orders to shoot to kill.

GEORGIE. Shooting? There's going to be shooting?

MR. BICKHARDT. Maybe not. That bellboy disguise should fool him good.

(*BABU reacts. GEORGIE reacts to what he's wearing.*)

GEORGIE. Oh, good. That's why I'm wearing this.

MR. BICKHARDT. Be on the lookout. He's dressed in black, with stringy black hair, a big mustache and eyes that have no soul.

(*Behind them, BABU reacts to his wardrobe and exits out the door SR.*)

GEORGIE. I'll be on the alert. Thank you.

MR. BICKHARDT. I could send a couple of guys to take turns watching you if it'll make you feel better.

GEORGIE. No! Absolutely not. Agent Heather is at the top of her field.

WALLY. Agent Heather?

HEATHER. (*Enters.*) All dry.

MR. BICKHARDT. What do you have? 44's or 38's?

HEATHER. I beg your pardon!

GEORGIE. (*Sotto.*) I'm sorry. He's such a pig. He's my brother's shower-pal.

MR. BICKHARDT. I was just saying, I'd like to send up a few men to take turns with you in case you want to get some sleep.

HEATHER. What?

MR. BICKHARDT. Three guys could rotate with him.

HEATHER. What?

MR. BICKHARDT. It would actually be pretty exciting for them. They've never gotten close to action like this.

HEATHER. Oh, please. He has enough problems.

MR. BICKHARDT. I'm just thinking of him. It might make him feel better.

HEATHER. I'm sure you mean will, but . . .

MR. BICKHARDT. Say, where do you put your protection?

HEATHER. I beg your pardon.

MR. BICKHARDT. Didn't mean to pry into official business. (*To Wally.*) Let's go, you.

WALLY. Your wish is my command.

(*BICKHARDT and WALLY exit with cart.*)

HEATHER. Where are they going?

GEORGIE. To take another shower together. He's such an embarrassment to the family. Let's get out of here!

MISSY. (*Enters from SR.*) I'm back! Did they catch that evil psycho?

GEORGIE. Uh . . . yes. All caught. Heather and I were just leaving. Weren't we, Heather?

HEATHER. Who is this?

MISSY. I'm Missy Ffrench. With two "fs." Ever heard of me?

HEATHER. No.

MISSY. (*Pats Heather on the head.*) You're little Heather? I've heard so much about you.

HEATHER. (*Bashful.*) You have?

MISSY. My, you're an awfully big girl.

HEATHER. I'm retaining a little water.

GEORGIE. It's a glandular thing.

(*WALLY runs in. HE can barely speak HE is so out of breath.*)

WALLY. Headed this way! Black boots. Black coat. Stringy hair. Mustache! Hide!

(*ALL panic and run around in circles. GEORGIE and WALLY run into each other and fall down.*)

HEATHER. Who is it? Feds?

MISSY. (*To Georgie.*) Remember to die in my arms.

WALLY & GEORGIE. Okay.

GEORGIE. (*As WALLY reacts.*) Get down!

(*POUNDING on the door.*)

HEATHER. What's that?

WALLY. It ain't opportunity.

MISSY. Quick the bathroom!

HEATHER. There's water all over the floor in there! I don't think your brother and his shower-buddy used the bath mat!

MISSY. (*To Wally.*) What?

WALLY. No time! Hit the floor!

(*ALL dive on the floor next to the bed. With Georgie DSR corner of the bed, Wally DSL corner of the bed, Heather USL corner of the bed, and Missy USR corner of the bed, ALL pull the spread out over their heads so it looks like a King-size well-made bed. ARLENE rushes in. SHE is spitting nails.*)

ARLENE. I called you office you little slimy rat-puking weasel. You're here with that bimbo secretary. You're both dead meat! (*SHE opens the closet.*) I'll rip you apart limb from limb. Limb from limb. Vein by vein. Vein by vein. (*SHE heads for bathroom.*) When I get through with you two . . . you'll have to . . . Whoooaaa!!

(*SFX: ARLENE slips and falls in the bathroom. EVERYONE pops out of the bed.*)

> WALLY. Let's get out of here!
> HEATHER. What's she doing here?
> GEORGIE. Trying to kill me!
> HEATHER. My God, you have problems coming out of your ears!

(*ALL rise. THEY hear KEYS at the front door.*)

> GEORGIE. Somebody's coming!

(*WALLY gets into the bed. GEORGIE dives into the bed under the covers, leaving his shoes exposed DS. It appears as if Georgie's feet are actually Wally's. MISSY and HEATHER hide behind US drapes, as MR. BICKHARDT rushes in.*)

> MR. BICKHARDT. What's going on in here? Someone said they saw a suspicious looking person headed this way.
> WALLY. Nobody here but li'l ol' me.

(*The adjoining room door DSL opens and the GUEST enters in his bathrobe and pajamas.*)

GUEST. What's a man got to do to get some peace and quiet in this hotel?

MR. BICKHARDT. There's no noise coming from here. This room is empty!

GUEST. I'm telling you. It's a regular nightclub in here!

MR. BICKHARDT. I'm Terrence Bickhardt, the Hotel Manager, and I'll take care of it immediately, sir. Wally, get out of that bed.

WALLY. Oh, do I have to?

MR. BICKHARDT. Wally, get up from there.

(*BICKHARDT tugs on his feet, which are really Georgie's feet.*)

WALLY. Ow, you're stretching my leg!

(*BICKHARDT pulls Georgie's feet even farther.*)

GUEST. Jesus! Stop that!
WALLY. Yow!!

(*BICKHARDT twists Georgie's feet around and it looks like Wally's body has been cut in half.*)
GUEST. You people are crazy!

(*BICKHARDT drops Georgie's feet. They lie all twisted in relation to Wally's body. The GUEST runs out to his room.*)

MR. BICKHARDT. (*To Wally.*) Get out of that bed or you're fired. Hey, where's Fish?

(*Offstage NOISE of Arlene rising and "Whooooaaa" falling again.*)

MR. BICKHARDT. Is that Fish?
WALLY. Don't let the aroma fool you.

(*BICKHARDT heads for the bathroom. WALLY jumps out of bed to cut him off. Georgie's legs disappear under the bed.*)

WALLY. I wouldn't do that if I were you.
MR. BICKHARDT. (*Exiting to bathroom.*) Fish? (*Looking off.*) Ah!!
WALLY. (*Looking off.*) God, there's water and fat everywhere!
MR. BICKHARDT. (*Shaking Wally.*) The terrorist! Run for your life!
WALLY. (*Shaking Bickhardt.*) Look out! Shamu's rising out of the water!

(*The GUEST pops back in. He sees WALLY and BICKHARDT shaking each other in fear.*)

GUEST. What the hell are you doing to him now?
MR. BICKHARDT. Run for your life!

(*BICKHARDT tramples the Guest as HE exits out the DSL door.*)

GUEST. (*Following.*) Hey! Get out of my room!

(*The GUEST exits DSL as ARLENE runs in from the bathroom rubbing her head.*)

ARLENE. Where is he? I'll punch him so hard, blood will shoot out his pants.
WALLY. (*Waving to front door.*) Bye, Georgie . . . I mean, (*Stops waving, pretends HE'S covering.*) hello Arlene!
ARLENE. (*Squishing Wally's face in her hands.*) Where did he go?
WALLY. I don't know. But it sure wasn't up on (*Pointedly.*) *the roof!*
ARLENE. The roof! (*Following after "Georgie."*) Come back here you wet little scab!

(*ARLENE runs out the front door. ALL climb out of their hiding spots.*)

HEATHER. What's she doing here?
MISSY. From all the photos I've seen on the news, I thought she was a man.
GEORGIE. A lot of people get that mixed up.
HEATHER. What news reports?
MISSY. She's killed thousands single-handedly.

HEATHER. She has? (*To Georgie.*) Why didn't you ever tell me any of this?

GEORGIE. I didn't think it was important.

HEATHER. (*To Georgie.*) Oh, Mr. Leach . . . all these years I thought you were just shy. But you were sparing my life!

GEORGIE. I was?

HEATHER. I should have put two and two together. I can't believe how naive I can be sometimes. I thought you liked me, but my girlfriends just said you either had asthma or head lice.

GEORGIE. They did? I mean, you do? Oh, Heather, the things I've wanted to tell you . . .

WALLY. Now? You pick now to have this discussion? Let's go!!

HEATHER. I don't want to get you killed! I love you!

MISSY. Well, of course you don't, honey. Who will be there to watch you graduate?

GEORGIE. Did you say you loved me?

(*THEY kiss.*)

MISSY, What a wonderful relationship he has with his daughter. (*SHE reacts to the long kiss.*) Hey, hey! There are laws! Cut it out!

WALLY. Let's get out of here!

(*THEY all head for the door as BABU RASHAAD enters, dressed as a bellhop. ALL back up into*

*the room. GEORGIE and WALLY squint and
do doubletakes.)*

BABU. Rooming service.

GEORGIE & WALLY. Arlene?

BABU. Rooming service.

GEORGIE. (*Sotto.*) Wally . . . does this guy
work here?

WALLY. (*Sotto.*) I've never seen him before
in my life.

GEORGIE. (*Sotto.*) Omigod. Keep my
memory alive, Heather.

HEATHER. Who is he?

WALLY. Goodbye, Georgie.

GEORGIE. Goodbye, Wally. And thanks for
getting me this room.

BABU. (*To Wally.*) You are him? Dressed a
bell-bottom boy.

WALLY. I are not him. I wish you guys would
learn the language. If you're gonna work in our
country . . .

BABU. (*To Georgie, who shields his face.*)
You are he?

GEORGIE. No. I'm no he.

BABU. You are he! You are he!

WALLY. (*Correcting him.*) "Him!" "I am
him!"

BABU. (*Drawing dagger.*) Aha!

WALLY. No! I mean, I am no he.

HEATHER. Mr. Fish, what is going on?

BABU. (*Turning dagger on Georgie.*) Aha!

GEORGIE. I'm not Mr.Fish!

HEATHER. But that's what you told me to call you!

MISSY. He's not Mr. Fish. He's Mr. Leach.

GEORGIE. It's all right, Heather. Tell him who I really am.

HEATHER. Mr. Fish.

GEORGIE. See? I'm Mr. . . . no! Mr. Fish . . . has a big mustache!

BABU. He has no such mustache!

GEORGIE. Yes . . . but I do. (*Rips out a chunk of Wally's hair, which HE sticks on his lip.*)

WALLY. Ow!

MISSY. (*Sotto.*) Get him, Wally. It's Babu!

WALLY. I know. And it's bleeding.

(*STAN and ROGER enter in their bellboy uniforms.*)

ROGER. Now we do the even numbers!

STAN. (*To Roger.*) Stop making me carry the heavy ones . . .

(*ROGER points out the others to Stan. BABU grabs Georgie and puts the dagger in his ribs.*)

BABU. (*Sotto.*) One move and you die.

STAN. Who are you people?

BABU. We are from rooming service. More towels you'll be needing?

STAN. Against the wall. All of you men. And spread'em!

HEATHER. (*To Georgie.*) Is he a friend of your brother's?

(*ALL move to walls hands raised. STAN starts frisking Wally.*)

WALLY. Hey, watch the tips.

MISSY. Where were you guys? Mr. Leach could've been killed!

ROGER. Who?

(*MISSY motions with her head to Babu.*)

ROGER. What's the matter with your head?

HEATHER. (*Sotto, to Missy.*) Who are they?

MISSY. CIA.

HEATHER. Certified Independent Accountants?

STAN. (*Frisking Georgie.*) You all better explain yourselves.

BABU. I am from rooming service.

STAN. (*Frisking Babu, removes pig mask and dagger.*) What's this? You dress up like farm animals to open your mail?

BABU. Yes.

MISSY. No! It's Babu!

(*EVERYONE panics. STAN sees Georgie's fake moustache and grabs him.*)

STAN. (*Aiming gun at Georgie.*) Start talking Babu. (*RE: his mustache.*) I know a clever disguise when I see one.

GEORGIE. This is not a disguise. (*Mustache falls off.*) Well, it is a disguise . . . but . . . you're gonna laugh when you hear this.

STAN. I like a good joke.

WALLY. Really? A guy's out duck hunting and he . . .

(*The GUEST returns, bursting in from his room.*)

GUEST. Will you shut up!!

(*STAN turns and shoots him. The GUEST slides down the wall.*)

GUEST. I should've said "please." (*Shuts his door.*)

STAN. Omigod!

(*STAN is stunned and drops his gun. BABU dives for it. HE holds it on the men.*)

BABU. You shall all die like fleas in a flame.

STAN. (*To Babu.*) You mean . . . you're not from rooming service?

WALLY. Good guess, Sherlock.

BABU. You leave me no choice. You will all die like the insolent dogs you are.

WALLY. And if we don't?

BABU. I just told you, you will all be shot like the insolent dogs you are.

ROGER. Wait a minute. I thought we were all dying like fleas in a flame.

WALLY. Either way we lose.

GEORGIE. Yeah, and it'll be like insolent dogs or burning fleas.

STAN. Oh, mommy.

HEATHER. We don't have the money.

MISSY. What money?

ROGER. Let the others go. I am Mr. Fish.

STAN. No, he's not. I am Mr. Fish.

GEORGIE. Well, don't look at me, 'cause I am no he!

WALLY. (*Points to Stan and Roger.*) It's one of those two guys. (*Singling out Stan.*) And I hope it's him!

BABU. Very well.

(*BABU starts to aim his gun at the men. BICKHARDT enters. BABU sticks his gun in Roger's ribs. Since he is closest. ALL the bellhops stand together as BICKHARDT enters.*)

MR. BICKHARDT. Good news. They've cornered him on the roof and . . Well, well, well. What are all you men doing here?

HEATHER. Oh, God. Do we have to watch this?

WALLY. Hi, Mr. Bickhardt.

(*WALLY steps out of line and crosses to Bickhardt, smiling at the ease of his safety. The other four MEN stand together.*)

HEATHER. He really does like that little one.

MR. BICKHARDT. Who are you men? You don't work for me.

(*GEORGIE, STAN, ROGER and BABU look for a way to explain themselves. The four MEN simultaneously break into "By the Light of the Silvery Moon."*)

WALLY. You damn conventioneers. Go back to your own rooms!

(*WALLY chases the four MEN off to the bathroom. HE grabs Missy and Heather and heads for the front door.*)

WALLY. (*To others.*) Well, I gotta go blow up balloons . . .

(*WALLY races out SR with his balloon cart, dragging Heather and Missy with him. The QUARTET enters from the bathroom, sings a*

*quick "encore" and exits into the bathroom
again where we hear all four MEN fall
offstage with four "WHOOOAA's" and four
CRASHES.)*

MR. BICKHARDT. Where's Mr. Fish?
ARLENE. (*Enters SR. Wiping hands and
chuckling to herself.*) That security guard
screamed like a girl.
MR. BICKHARDT. Black boots! Black coat!
Stringy hair! Mustache! Don't hurt me. Don't hurt
me. (*Runs out USR.*)
ARLENE. Men are so weak. I'll get what I
want if I have to stay here all night. Bellhop
lounge, my ass! (*Turns on radio.*)

(*SFX: "The Waltz from Swan Lake" plays.
ARLENE lounges on the bed.
The Bellhop Ballet: [All choreographed to the
waltz.]
GEORGIE creeps out of the bathroom, rubbing his
head. Sees Arlene and runs back into the
bathroom as SHE turns over in the bed.
HEATHER creeps in the front door in search of
Georgie. MISSY follows her quickly,
dragging her back out the door, as ARLENE
rolls over yet again.
STAN creeps by the window on the ledge SL
escaping from the bathroom. HE signals for
Roger to follow him.*

ROGER *appears on the ledge SL, crawling, scared to death. HE motions "No way" "Too high" as HE and STAN have an argument. ROGER rises, loses his balance and starts to fall backwards. STAN races from the SR window to the SL window and saves Roger. Taking Roger's hand, THEY creep off SR together.*

WALLY *enters front door with his party favor service cart – on which is tied a bunch of helium balloons and a helium cannister. HE sees Arlene stir and ducks into closest as:*

MISSY *enters from the adjoining room scaring Wally into the closet. SHE is followed by the GUEST who is wounded and orders her out of his room. SHE crosses in and the door closes, locking the GUEST out of his own room.*

BABU *backs out of the bathroom, rubbing his head. MISSY is startled into hiding behind the drapes. The GUEST sees Babu and leans against the wall SL.*

WALLY *opens closet door, sees Babu and shuts the door. The closing door startles BABU into ducking behind the upstage curtains, forcing MISSY to jump out and hide under the bed. BABU and WALLY have a peek-a-boo contest alternating between WALLY opening and closing the closet door, BABU peeking out and hiding behind the drapes, the GUEST peeking out and hiding against the SL wall, and MISSY popping in and out from the foot of the bed. ARLENE scratches in time to the music.*

GEORGIE appears on the ledge from SL, dizzy
and dazed. HE edges slowly. BABU sees him
go past the window he's hiding at, puts dagger
in his teeth, and tries opening the SL window
to follow him. GEORGIE sees BABU spy him
and quickly scurries to the SR window.

ARLENE stirs and sees Georgie on the ledge
outside the SR window. SHE rises and opens
the SR window to go after him. GEORGIE
panics and heads back the way HE came (SL).

BABU and ARLENE open their respective
windows and go out onto the ledge, EACH
headed towards center, with GEORGIE
somewhere in between them. BABU looks
menacing with his dagger between his teeth.
ARLENE looks maniacal with hands
outstretched. THEY disappear behind the
center wall.

The GUEST crawls off into the bathroom.
WALLY and MISSY change places. SHE
ends up in closet, HE under the bed.

ARLENE and BABU reappear in each other's
windows. ARLENE now has the dagger in her
teeth. THEY look behind them to see what
happened to GEORGIE who is nowhere to be
seen. ARLENE heads off SL, BABU heads off
SR.

As the music repeats the opening lines;

*STAN enters from the bathroom, unable to find
     Roger whom he thought was right behind him.
     HE goes back out to find him.*

*ROGER enters from the adjoining room, looking
     for Stan. HE exits back out in search of him.*

*STAN repeats the same moves, this time holding
     hands with the GUEST, who follows him.
     STAN talks to himself. The GUEST and
     STAN see each other and chase off into the
     bathroom.*

*ROGER repeats the same moves, talking to
     himself, making a circle with his hand to
     retrace his past steps. HE exits into the
     adjoining room to look for Stan.*

*GEORGIE hangs down from above the SL
     window, eyes bulging in terror. HE climbs
     down onto the ledge.*

*GEORGIE climbs in the SL window, making sure
     the coast is clear. HE checks out the window he
     just entered to be sure he wasn't followed.
     BABU backs from SR into the SR window.
     STAN backs in from bathroom USL. ROGER
     from the adjoining room DSL. ALL creep in to
     DSC without seeing each other. WALLY
     climbs out from under bed.*

ALL FIVE come together at center and scream.

*WALLY exits front door, slamming the door in
     Georgie's face. ROGER is pulled out
     adjoining room by STAN who slams that door
     in Georgie's face as well. GEORGIE pleads*

for his life at SL as BABU stalks him, dagger drawn.

MISSY appears from the closet. SHE desperately tries flirting with Babu CS to get him away from Georgie. As BABU turns his attention to Missy, GEORGIE tries tip-toeing past BABU, who grabs him by the shirt. HEATHER appears from the bathroom, sees MISSY flirting to save Georgie's life and tries flirting as well. BABU is torn between two women and killing Georgie.

The GUEST enters from the bathroom sees HEATHER flirting and decides he'll flirt with her as well. HEATHER shrugs him off to flirt with Babu. MISSY shimmies and wiggles with the music.

ARLENE appears at the front door scaring everyone. SHE sees Georgie and Heather and heads for them. GEORGIE uses the GUEST as a shield. HEATHER uses BABU as a shield. MISSY tries flirting to distract her, and ARLENE pushes her away. ARLENE pushes Babu aside. HEATHER runs out the bathroom. GEORGIE hiding behind the Guest signals to Arlene "He went that-away" pointing off USL. ARLENE exits into the bathroom USL. GEORGIE hugs the Guest for saving his life and crushes his "shot up" arm. HE runs off USL. Outside the US windows, ROGER and STAN go by SL to SR.

*BABU now has Georgie alone, draws his dagger
    and chases him around the room. On the
    second pass by the bed, BABU trips and MISSY
    dives on his back. BABU chases Georgie one
    time around with MISSY clinging to his back.
    On the third pass around the room, GEORGIE
    gets tired and sits at the SL chair, signaling
    for Babu to go on without him. BABU does.
    Then realizes what HE is doing. BABU
    dumps Missy on the bed and comes at Georgie.
    GEORGIE mashes him in the groin with the
    service cart.*

*BABU grabs the service cart. GEORGIE keeps it
    between them as HE and BABU spin in
    circles. The MUSIC BUILDS. MISSY grabs
    the tray off the rolling bar. SHE swings
    several times at BABU, but as THEY go faster
    and faster SHE can't tell Babu and Georgie
    apart.*

*MISSY readies the tray and guesses wrong –
    knocking GEORGIE out cold like a rag doll.*

*Before HE can hit the ground, from the front door
    comes ROGER chased by ARLENE. The
    GUEST enters DSL with MR. BICKHARDT,
    who is horrified by what HE sees. HEATHER
    enters from the bathroom. ROGER grabs
    Georgie as a rag doll shield and exits DSL.*

*HEATHER follows. ARLENE chases them off.
    The GUEST follows Arlene off DSL.*

*STAN enters USR, gun drawn. STAN follows
    after the GUEST. MISSY follows Stan, BABU*

follows STAN, and MR. BICKHARDT follows last. All of this is done in split seconds.

WALLY enters the front door in time to see this mass exodus. HE paces trying to think of a plan.

Suddenly on the ledge, running from SR we see Roger. WALLY gets an idea, and signals to open window SR. As ROGER climbs in and runs out the front door, WALLY gets helium cannister off the cart and readies himself on the bed.

One by one the OTHERS follow Roger in the SR window and out the front door – in this order: HEATHER, THE GUEST, STAN and MISSY.

MISSY yells and points off behind her towards SL. WALLY readies his cannister.

GEORGIE enters through the SR window coming in from the SR side. HE is knocked out cold by WALLY.

WALLY grabs Georgie's body and slumps it over the service cart wheeling him off to the bathroom, taking the helium balloons off the cart, getting a brilliant idea.

ARLENE enters the SR window behind Georgie, carrying Stan's gun. SHE is greeted by Mr. Bickhardt and a CIA agent who enter from USR. The AGENT knees her in the groin and carts her away. SHE protests her innocence.

BABU enters the adjoining room looking for Georgie. GEORGIE sails past the SL window on the bunch of helium balloons. He flies up and away, waving goodbye to Babu. WALLY enters from the bathroom wiping his hands. HE waves goodbye to Georgie.

BABU climbs out the SL window and tries diving after Georgie – swan diving to his "death" below. WALLY waves up in the sky to Georgie and waves down to Babu below, making a horrible face at what must have become of him. The MUSIC builds and ends. WALLY shuts the window, wipes his hands, yawns, and turns off the radio.

CURTAIN

END OF ACT I

ACT II

Curtain opens.
The same hotel room. Moments later.
WALLY, MISSY and HEATHER are seated and
sobbing.

HEATHER. Poor Mr. Leach . . .
MISSY. There, there. You can live with me.

(*MISSY puts her arm around Heather. SHE*
reacts.)

HEATHER. I don't want to live with you.
WALLY. It's all my fault.
MISSY. No, it isn't.
WALLY. Yes, it is.
MISSY. No, it isn't.
HEATHER. Yes, it is!
WALLY. Oh, sure, blame me! It seemed like
a good idea at the time. Who would've guessed all
those CIA agents would have opened fire like that
and riddled the balloons with bullets.
MISSY. (*Making a path of the deflated*
balloons.) He did do a lovely fleur-de-lis as all
the air gushed out.

74

(THEY all sob.)

HEATHER. I loved him so much I could barely tell him. All this over some stupid books.

MISSY. I know. I know. Well, at least he died for a cause.

HEATHER. Yes, but where did he stash all the money?

WALLY. Hey, my brother just died. Show a little respect.

(SR door opens and a lisping twelve year old girl, dressed as a bellboy enters.)

HEIDI. Room service.

WALLY. We didn't order any . . . hey, what is this? Did we order the children's portion?

MISSY. Can we help you, honey?

WALLY. What's the matter, Pippi? Lose your longstocking?

HEIDI. I'm Little Heidi. I'm looking for my father.

(MISSY and HEATHER look at the little bellboy, then look at Wally – dressed the same way.)

WALLY. Hey . . . I was no where near Cleveland, twelve years ago.

(MISSY slaps Wally.)

HEIDI. He's not my father! He could never be my father. That would be like saying . . . a man was "Pete Rose" just because he made a few bets and touched his privates.

HEATHER. What does that mean?

WALLY. (*Touching himself.*) I think she's saying that I'm not her father.

MISSY. Who is your father, honey?

HEIDI. Mr. Fish.

MISSY. Mith-der Fitsth?

HEIDI. Yes.

HEATHER. Oh, you mean . . . Mr. Leach?

MISSY. Yes.

HEIDI. No. Mr. "Fish."

MISSY. That's what she meant.

HEIDI. Where's my Daddy?

HEATHER. (*Glancing out window.*) Well . . . I don't know how to tell you this . . .

WALLY. We don't know where your father is, kid.

MISSY. He loop-de-looped the corner of 57th and 5th and we haven't seen him since.

(*GEORGIE appears in the window, covered with remnants of ripped balloons and bird feathers. HE is terrified and wobbly.*)

GEORGIE. (*In a helium-induced voice.*) Help me . . . help me . . . help me . . .

(*THEY help him.*)

WALLY. He's alive! He's alive! Look, he's alive!

MISSY. (*To Heather and Heidi.*) Look, it's your father.

HEIDI. Huh?

(*GEORGIE wobbles in, HE's too weak to stand, and WALLY helps him steady himself.*)

WALLY. What happened? We thought you were dead!

GEORGIE. They shot my balloons! All the helium gushed out and I zoomed all over town . . . I flew around Central Park . . . right through a flock of pigeons . . . I almost neutered myself on the top of the Chrysler building . . . And then suddenly . . . coming right at me . . . was the lowest airplane I ever saw. It came closer and closer and closer. I screamed. "Alter your course! Alter your course!" But it flew right at me. Close enough until I saw a psychotic glint in the pilot's eye as he barreled down on me. And I kept screaming . . . "Alter your course! You're headed right towards me! Alter your course! Alter your course! Alter your course!!"

WALLY. What happened?

GEORGIE. (*Casually.*) He altered his course.

WALLY. How'd you get back here?

GEORGIE. I don't know. I hit an awning and next thing I knew I flew face first into a window washer on the twenty-third floor. I never heard a man scream like that before.

WALLY. The poor guy.

GEORGIE. The man screaming was me.

HEATHER. (*Smothering him with a kiss.*) So, you're all right?

GEORGIE. Yeah, but I got bugs in my teeth.

(*HEATHER reacts.*)

MISSY. But you're all right, Mr. Fish?

GEORGIE. Yes . . .

HEIDI. Mr. Fish? You're not my father!! What did you do with my father?

(*HEIDI gives Georgie a swift kick in the shins.*)

GEORGIE. Ow!

MISSY. You're not Roger Fish?

GEORGIE. No. I'm Georgie Leach!

MISSY. (*Slaps him.*) You lied to me, just so you could take advantage of my big plan to become famous!

HEATHER. (*Slaps him.*) You took advantage of her?

WALLY. (*Slaps him.*) Hey, she's *my* girl.

GEORGIE. I didn't take advantage of anybody.

*(GEORGIE walks away. MISSY slaps Wally
thinking Georgie is still in the same place.)*

MISSY. No, but you meant to.
WALLY. Hey!
GEORGIE. I never said I was Roger Fish. *You*
said I was Roger Fish!
MISSY. Then who are you? And what are you
doing in this room?
GEORGIE. I'm Georgie Leach! And I came
here to have an affair with my . . . my . . . *(Sees
Heather.)* My-my! You look pretty today.
MISSY. Leach? You're Wally's brother?
WALLY. That's what I tried telling you.
HEATHER. I already knew that. He's that
prissy man's soap slave.
WALLY. What?
HEIDI. Where's my father?

(Little HEIDI kicks Georgie in the shins.)

WALLY. What's he look like, kid?
HEIDI. He looks like my father!
WALLY. Ask a stupid question.

*(Little HEIDI kicks Wally as ARLENE bursts in.
SHE leans against the door, seething through
gritted teeth.)*

MISSY. It's the terrorist! Run for your lives.

(*MISSY, HEIDI and WALLY run around in fear.*)

GEORGIE. Arlene's not a terrorist!

(*THEY stop running around.*)

WALLY. Yeah, but she's no picnic, either. (*Continues running around in fear.*)

MISSY. (*Stopping.*) If she's not a terrorist, then who is she?

GEORGIE. (*Softly.*) My . . . wife.

MISSY. Your what?

GEORGIE. My wife, "Arlene." Arlene, Missy Ffrench.

MISSY. With two "fs." Ever heard of me?

ARLENE. No.

GEORGIE. And, of course, you know Heather.

ARLENE. Those CIA clowns thought I was an assassin. They frisked me. They fingerprinted me. They strip-searched me. I showed them! I sweat all over their hands.

WALLY. Did you say sweat? Or . . . never mind.

ARLENE. (*To Georgie.*) Well, well, well. What have we here?

GEORGIE. This isn't what it looks like, dear.

ARLENE. It looks like you're having a pathetic affair with your bow-legged secretary.

HEATHER. Now, just a minute . . .

MISSY. Secretary? I thought she was your daughter.

ARLENE. Then you're even stupider than your name.

GEORGIE. What are you going to do with us?

ARLENE. Nothing. Just give me my money and I'll leave.

HEATHER. Money?

ARLENE. I saw you leave the house with it today.

GEORGIE. What money?

ARLENE. Don't play innocent with me or I'll pull your lip up over your head and tuck it in the back of your pants!

HEATHER. The $500,000?

GEORGIE. That's what you're looking for?

ARLENE. Where is it?

GEORGIE. You stole $500,000 from Bendetson, Bendetson and Howard?

ARLENE. What do you think I came to your office for? To visit *you?* Now tell me where it is, or I'll pummel it out of you.

GEORGIE. No. No! Not like our honeymoon . . .

(*ARLENE takes Georgie and punches him in the stomach three times, sending him high up in the air on each punch.*)

GEORGIE. Wally . . .
HEATHER. Oh!

GEORGIE. Cut it out! You're bursting my appendix!

WALLY. I don't want to watch this. Turn away, Little Heidi.

GEORGIE. (*To Arlene.*) I don't have $500,000.

ARLENE. (*As SHE chokes Georgie.*) Are you going to talk?

GEORGIE. (*In a strangled voice.*) I am talking . . . Can't you hear me? I don't have any money. Wally had to sneak me into this room because I couldn't afford it on my own.

WALLY. And it was my pleasure, too. Let me tell you.

MISSY. Wally, do something!

WALLY. What for? She doesn't need any help.

(*ARLENE throws Georgie across the room. HE lies in a heap. ARLENE starts rummaging through the room.*)

GEORGIE. I'll give you my watch . . .

WALLY. (*Gets an idea. To Arlene.*) Georgie had the money when he left the house today?

ARLENE. You catch on fast, you drooling idiot!

MISSY. He isn't drooling.

(*WALLY whispers to Heidi. HEIDI heads for the door.*)

ARLENE. And where do you think you're going, Munchkin Man?

HEIDI. Call for Phillip Morris. Call for Phillip Morris. (*Exits.*)

ARLENE. Since when did this hotel start hiring side-show freaks?

WALLY. Hey, is that any way to talk about Little Heidi?

ARLENE. I was talking about you, you freak.

(*STAN and ROGER enter.*)

STAN. Don't worry about a thing, Mr. Fish. In 36 hours your daughter will be an official missing person and . . .

ROGER. 36 hours?

STAN. (*Sees Arlene.*) It's him! Stand back!

(*STAN throws Roger backwards over a chair. HE pulls out his pistol, which flies away. He picks it up.*)

STAN. Hit the floor, everyone!

(*ALL but Stan and Arlene hit the floor.*)

STAN. Up against the wall, you freedom-hating violence-monger.

(*STAN kicks Arlene in the crotch and throws her against the wall to frisk her.*)

ARLENE. Hey, hey, hey . . .

STAN. (*Stopping.*) Uh oh. (*Sniffs.*) Mrs. Leach? Gosh, I'm sorry.

ARLENE. Didn't you have enough fun downstairs? Shall we tell them what I had to show you to prove I was a woman?

(*ALL begin to rise.*)

WALLY. Please don't. I may vomit.

HEATHER. Are you all right, Mr. Leach?

GEORGIE. I fell on the big buttons.

ROGER. You're lucky. I fell on my mechanical pencil. And the tip is still up there.

STAN. (*To Arlene.*) Sorry, our men mistook you for that brutal Babu Rashaad, Mrs. Leach. You *are* dressed just like him. All in black. Same hair. Same musta -- . . . Same hair.

(*Behind them, a disheveled Babu, hatless and desperate, climbs up onto the ledge.*)

WALLY. You don't have to worry about that guy. He took a nosedive off the ledge right after you accidentally arrested Arlene.

ROGER. He did?

(*BABU starts to open the window.*)

WALLY. Check downstairs. He's probably some cabbie's hood ornament by now.

STAN. Terrorism is never pretty.

ROGER. Then . . . I'm safe?

STAN. Guess so. I'll call downstairs and call off my CIA dogs.

(*BABU climbs in the SL window. HE picks up the bag HE entered with earlier and removes a bomb.*)

BABU. I am leaving no choicing but to destroy everyone!

(*ALL gasp.*)

ARLENE. A lot of help you've been.

STAN. Easy, Mrs. Leach.

BABU. You will all suffer like the red ants make the snake suffer.

ARLENE. Hey, I've suffered enough.

GEORGIE. Arlene! That's . . .

ARLENE. (*Sees bomb.*) What the hell have you got there? What kind of a man carries a purse? What is this? (*Grabs the bomb.*)

BABU. No! It is . . .

ARLENE. It looks like a . . .

BABU. Bomb.

ARLENE. . . . bomb. (*Freezes.*) Bomb? (*To Heather.*) Isn't he your husband?

HEATHER. No! I'm a bachelor girl!

ARLENE. Then he's . . .
ALL. Babu.
ARLENE. You mean . . .
ALL. The terrorist!
BABU. I am Babu Rashaad!
ARLENE. Ah!

(*ARLENE panics and throws bomb to Stan.*)

STAN. Nobody move.

(*EVERYBODY runs around.*)

STAN. Freeze! I told you to freeze! It's ticking!

(*ALL freeze.*)

BABU. You pulled-ed starter. Two minutes to booming noise.
ROGER. Call the booming squad. I mean, call the bomb . . .
STAN. There's no time.
BABU. (*Shaking Georgie.*) I must not die. I was sent by the Obodanza of La Banza. I am on a mission from the gods.
GEORGIE. I am no he!
MISSY. What do we do now?
STAN. (*Handing bomb to Roger.*) Hold this for a minute. (*To Others.*) Anybody have a watch?

GEORGIE. I do. But the second hand doesn't work right. It sticks on the nine.

ROGER. Hey!!

STAN. Oh, sorry.

ROGER. Somebody take this! (*Throws it to Babu.*)

BABU. Do not give me live bomb. I have done nothing. I shall live! (*Tosses it to Wally.*)

WALLY. Hey, pal. *I'm* not ready to go. I've still got three subway tokens to use up. (*Tosses it to Georgie.*)

GEORGIE. I am no he. (*Tosses it to Missy.*)

MISSY. I'm not famous enough yet. (*Tosses it to Heather.*)

HEATHER. (*Shyly.*) I'm still a virgin.

ALL. Really?

(*A fast game of hot potato starts.*)

STAN. (*To Georgie.*) Don't give it to me.

GEORGIE. (*To Missy.*) I don't want it.

MISSY. (*To Roger.*) I don't want it.

ROGER. (*To Arlene.*) You take it.

ARLENE. (*To Wally.*) I don't want it.

WALLY. (*To Arlene.*) Oh, go ahead and take it.

ARLENE. (*To Wally.*) Get it away from me.

WALLY. (*To Arlene.*) Come on, you could afford to lose a few pounds.

ARLENE. (*To Roger.*) Here, honey.

ROGER. Kemrite! What should we do with this?

(*ROGER throws it to Stan. The pattern becomes back and forth between STAN and EVERYONE ELSE as the GUEST enters from his room. He wears his bathrobe and pajamas, but his shoulder and arm are in a sling.*)

GUEST. I have been patient. I have been tolerant. I have been polite. But I demand. Do you hear me . . . demand . . . absolute quiet! And I want it now!!

STAN. Okay.

(*STAN throws the bomb to the GUEST, who backs into his room.*
SFX: BOMB EXPLODES.
As it explodes, PLASTER and SMOKE shoot out the door.)

HEATHER. Oh, the poor man.

MISSY. Poor man? Think of the maid who has to clean up in there!

STAN. (*To Babu.*) Well, I hope you're happy now.

ROGER. Look what you've done!

BABU. (*Going for Roger.*) It is most unfortunate. Now you see the destruction your book has wrought.

ROGER. My book? Just a minute. Just a cotton-picking minute. How did my book cause that man's death?

BABU. If you had not written the book which offended the Obodanza of La Banza, I would not have been send here, I would not have bring the bomb and the man would not have been blown with bits.

WALLY. (*To Roger.*) Well, if he explains it like that, I guess it *is* your fault.

ROGER. What?

ARLENE. Why don't we just blow his brains out?

GEORGIE. You can't do that!

ROGER. Of course not. In this country, we don't kill people like animals for expressing different points of view.

WALLY. Except at hockey games.

ROGER. (*To Babu.*) I am sick to death of people like you. If you hate my book – don't buy it. Don't read it. Don't give it cheap publicity by condemning it so loudly. Every man born on this planet has the right to think for himself, and speak for himself, and to write for himself. And if you don't agree with my opinions, well, that's your right as well. But if you censor our words, you censor our thoughts. And then we'll find ourselves unable to think for ourselves, to question, to criticize, to learn, to better ourselves, our civilizations, our futures and all of mankind suffers.

(*BABU just stares. The OTHERS are hushed.*)

ROGER. Wait. I'm not making myself clear. Let me put it this way. Let's say you're at a car dealership and . . . no, never mind that one. Let's say you want some ice cream . . .

MISSY. Oh, and he was doing so well.

BABU. You naive capitalist fat cats. In my country you would be eaten alive by wild boars and left stacked to a stick to rot in the sun until the birds pecked your eyes from their sockets.

(*STAN knees Babu in the groin.*)

STAN. Lucky for you, this is a kinder, gentler nation. (*Handcuffing him.*) Let's go, Babu. You've got an appointment across town. To spend the rest of your life in a little six by six foot cubicle with a sweat-stained bug-ridden mattress, a dirty little rusty sink and a hard slab floor — fenced in by thick iron bars.

BABU. In my country, this is what you call "condominium."

ARLENE. I still think you should have blown his brains out.

MR. BICKHARDT. (*Enters. To Georgie.*) I have a surprise for you, Mr. Fish. You'll never guess who I found rummaging through the coat check downstairs.

GEORGIE. I'm . . . I'm not Mr. Fish.

WALLY. Surprise.

ROGER. *I* am Roger Fish.

MR. BICKHARDT. What? (*To Wally.*) Explain this, Leach.

GEORGIE. Well . . .

WALLY. It was all my idea. I didn't want you to know he was in here . . . so . . .

MR. BICKHARDT. So you had this man pretend to be Mr. Fish, in case anyone found Mr. Fish was in this room?

WALLY. Er . . . yeah.

STAN. You did?

MR. BICKHARDT. Clever. Very clever.

WALLY. I thought you'd like it.

HEATHER. Oh, Mr. Leach. I'm so proud of you.

MR. BICKHARDT. Bring her in. O'Shannon.

(*"NUMBER FIVE" enters behind Heidi, who carries Georgie's suitcase.*)

HEIDI. Daddy!

ROGER. Little Heidi!

MR. BICKHARDT. Surprise!

(*THEY embrace.*)

ROGER. (*To Heidi.*) I was so afraid something had happened to you. It was as if . . . I were a greyhound in a dog race . . . and every time I got close to the mechanical rabbit . . . they'd lengthen the track . . .

HEIDI. I was scared, Daddy. Being locked in that hotel room was like I was . . . squeezed into a lunchbox . . . and every time I tried to eat my sandwich, I had to climb over the thermos.

ROGER. Oh, honey. I was going crazy trying to find you. It was as if I were on an escalator and...

GEORGIE. Oh, cut it out, will you?

BABU. Are you sure I cannot kill him? In my country the tongues of men are ripped from their throat who tell such long-winded stories.

ARLENE. (*Pounces on the suitcase.*) Hey! Give me that suitcase, you little juvenile delinquent. (*Snatching it away.*) I spent ten years building this little nest egg and I'm not about to lose it all now.

GEORGIE. $500,000. I'm gonna lose my job. Mr. Bendetson will kill me. And that's nothing compared to what Mr. Bendetson will do!

ARLENE. My heart really breaks for you. I'll send you a postcard from Buenos Aires.

GEORGIE. But . . . what about me?

ARLENE. I don't want you. Hasta la vista, schmuck.

(*ARLENE starts for the door. STAN blocks her way, gun drawn.*)

STAN. Not so fast, Mrs. Leach. I'll be taking that suitcase. Embezzling is a big offense, and I'm pretty sure it's punishable by law.

ARLENE. Go ahead. (*Opens empty suitcase.*) Can't arrest me for an empty suitcase, can you?

STAN. (*Looks through his manual.*) I guess not. (*Putting gun away.*) Sorry, Mr. Leach.

BABU. In my country you can arrest someone for an empty suitcase.

MISSY. Do something, Wally.

(*WALLY accidentally on purpose opens a secret compartment and money spills out.*)

WALLY. Oh, whoops, Arlene. Gee, what have I uncovered here?

ARLENE. You chewed up little piece of worm...

(*ARLENE tries picking up the cash. STAN holds the gun on her.*)

STAN. Well, I guess Babu has a cellmate to break rocks with in the Big House.

BABU. Have mercy!

MR. BICKHARDT. This is so exciting!

ARLENE. Georgie, don't let them take me . . . Georgie . . . I've always loved you, Georgie. Georgie? Say something!

GEORGIE. Hasta your own la vista, Arlene.

(*GEORGIE and HEATHER embrace as STAN leads Arlene and Babu out.*)

STAN. Coming, Mr. Fish? You'll be safer with me. (*Drops gun, retrieves it.*)

ROGER. I don't need protection anymore, Mr. Kemrite.

STAN. There are a lot more psychos out there than these two.

ROGER. What good is a man's freedom if he's not free to enjoy it? It would be like . . . say . . . I grew good tomato plants . . . and . . .

(*ALL groan.*)

STAN. Goodbye, Mr. Fish. Sorry I never got to make you my moussaka.

ROGER. (*Disappointed.*) Oh, and I love Greek food . . I mean . . .

BABU. Oh, Mr. Fish? Religion aside, I enjoyed your book.

ROGER. Thank you.

(*"NUMBER FIVE" takes Babu away.*)

ARLENE. (*To Georgie and Wally.*) You better hope I never get out. I'll be your worst nightmare.

WALLY. You're my worst nightmare now.

STAN. I bet I get a special badge for this.

(*STAN exits with Arlene in tow.*)

MR. BICKHARDT. You might want to use the back entrance, Mr. Fish. TV reporters are swarming all over the hotel. They got wind you were here. You're quite the talk of the town. And now with the capture of that maniac, they'll really go crazy.

ROGER. They will? Come on, Little Heidi. A little TV publicity might make a few people actually read my book.

HEIDI. Yeah. It could be like when you're forced to play with the nerdy kid next door and he lets you feel his muscles.

ROGER. Yeah. Yeah. Or when you're forced to eat liver and as you choke on it, it starts to taste really good.

(*ROGER and HEIDI exit.*)

MR. BICKHARDT. (*To Wally.*) You're a hero, Wally. You helped snare that terrorist and that embezzler. I'm proud to have you on my staff. . . carrying people's soiled linens, and clearing dirty food-encrusted dishes.

WALLY. It's what I live for, Mr. Bickhardt.

MR. BICKHARDT. How does "The Head of Security" sound?

WALLY. (*In a deep voice.*) He's got a deep voice like this.

MR. BICKHARDT. No, I mean . . . How does "Wally Leach, The Head of Security" sound?

MISSY. (*Embracing him.*) Oh, Wally. You've always wanted to say, "Yes, that *is* a gun in my pocket."

GEORGIE. Congratulations, brother.

WALLY. Does it pay more than what I make now ?

MR. BICKHARDT. My goodness, yes. Of course.

WALLY. Then I love it.

(*The GUEST enters from his room. His face is black from gunpowder. His hair stands on end. He wears remnants of his former clothing. He is covered in soot. HE carries a blown-up suitcase. When he speaks, SMOKE comes out of his mouth.*)

GUEST. I'll be checking out now.

MR. BICKHARDT. Very good. I hope you had a pleasant stay.

GUEST. Lovely. You might want to plug up the skylight before it rains again.

MR. BICKHARDT. What skylight? That room has no skylight.

GUEST. It does now. And the guests from the room above me keep coming in my room.

MR. BICKHARDT. Why should they do that?

GUEST. They have no floor. Has anyone seen my wife?

(*ALL react as the GUEST exits. BICKHARDT follows.*)

MR. BICKHARDT. Now, see here, sir. You can't leave the room in that condition. You are responsible for those damages. Are you with some heavy metal band? Come back here . . . (*Exits.*)

GEORGIE. (*Embracing Heather.*) We're finally alone.

HEATHER. Oh, Georgie. I can call you Georgie, can't I?

GEORGIE. I've dreamt of it for years.

(*THEY kiss.*)

MISSY. (*Embracing Wally.*) Oh, Wally. You're a hero. You're a regular celebrity.

WALLY. (*Modestly.*) I know.

(*THEY kiss.*)

MISSY. Hey . . . you could help me become a famous actress.

WALLY. How?

MISSY. Well . . .

(*MISSY whispers in Wally's ear. HE blushes.*)

WALLY. (*Pushing Georgie.*) Get the hell out of here, Georgie.

GEORGIE. Hey, not now.

WALLY. (*Pushing him to adjoining room.*) Now. Go use the room next door.

GEORGIE. There's no ceiling in there.

WALLY. (*Pushing Georgie and Heather out.*) That's all right. The people above you don't walk around very much.

GEORGIE. But there's plaster . . . there's schrapnel . . .

HEATHER. Oh, I love schrapnel . . .

(*HEATHER takes Georgie by the hand and pulls him off.*)

WALLY. (*To Missy.*) Don't worry, honey. Wally Leach is gonna make you a star.

(*As THEY embrace, behind them on the ledge we see HEATHER run into the SL window screaming in terror. SHE runs off SR. GEORGIE follows in each window shouting for help and running off R. THEY are followed by three terrorists who wear the "colors." All three are in black robes with black turbans, one with a black beard, one with a long grey mustache, one with an eye patch. One carries a dagger, one a pistol, one a club. THEY chase Georgie and Heather off SR.)*

CURTAIN CLOSES

END OF PLAY

COSTUMES

GEORGIE: Drab accountant's suit, white shirt, tie, dress shoes, black socks, garters, boxers, large white T-shirt
                   into
ill-fitting red bellhop uniform with black pants and red hat

WALLY: Red bellhop uniform, black pants, black shoes, red hat

BABU: Black turtleneck, black pants, long black coat, black boots, one large gold earring
                   into
red bellhop uniform, black pants, red hat

ARLENE: Black shirt, black pants, long black coat (duster), black high-heeled boots, two large gold earrings, fat suit under if needed

ROGER: Sports shirt, cardigan sweater, slacks, T-shirt, loafers
                   into
red bellhop uniform, black pants, red hat

STAN: Navy blazer, grey pants, white shirt, blue tie, mirrored aviator sunglasses, black shoes
                   into
red bellhop uniform, black pants, red hat

MISSY: Black french maid uniform, frilly white apron & cap, black tights, black high heels, black full slip

HEATHER: Red and white "sailor-type" dress, red shoes, red purse

BICKHARDT: Pinstriped suit, white shirt, red tie, name tag

GUEST: Red & black checkered bathrobe, white pajamas, Shriner's fez
                              into
"Bomb" exploded version of same

LITTLE HEIDI: Red bellhop uniform, black pants, red hat

NUMBER FIVE: Navy blazer, white shirt, grey pants, blue tie, black shoes, mirrored aviator sunglasses

PROPERTY LIST

Radio, Telephone, Ice Bucket, Water Pitcher, Glasses, "Do Not Disturb" sign, Crepe Hair, Bottle of Champagne, Small designer shopping bag, Silk pajamas, Roll of electrical tape, Overnight suitcase, Play money, Heart-shaped candy box, Flowers, "Satanic Nurses" novel, Shredded grey pants, Hanger, Dry cleaning wrapping, 5 Bellhop suitcases, Metal service cart, Balloons/Metallic (2 sets), Plastic helium canister, Large silver tray, 2 Terry hotel towels, Blank gun, Identical cap gun, CIA manual, Pocketknife, Dagger, Pig mask, Bomb, Guest suitcase, Bandages, Cigarettes, Lighter, Bird feathers, Deflated balloons, Hotel keys, Pass key on chain, Grilled salmon, Tablecloth, Room service place setting, Pencils, Vase of flowers, Rolling bar, Black bag.

PROPERTY PRE-SET LIST

Onstage:
Bed: Made
SR Night Table: Telephone
Bureau: Radio, Flowers
Door: "Do Not Disturb" sign

Off SR (Front Door):
Rolling Bar: Ice bucket, Water pitcher (filled),
Two glasses, (filled 1/8), Champagne, Silver tray
Shopping Bag: Silk pajamas, roll of electrical
    tape
Overnight Case: Flowers, Heart-shaped candy,
    false back with $500,000 money
Novel
Service cart with fish dinner set-up
Grey pants on hanger covered in dry cleaning
    plastic
5 Suitcases

Extras for Prop Table:
Cluster of metallic balloons
Helium canister
Extra crepe hair
Bomb in black bag
Deflated balloons
Bird feathers

Bathroom SL:
2 Terry cloth towels

Off DSR:
Bandages
Cigarettes
Lighter
Guest Suitcase

Out Window:
Helium Balloon gag rigged and re-set to SL
　　position

PERSONAL:
GEORGIE: Crepe hair in bellhop pocket
STAN: Gun, CIA manual, pocketknife
ROGER: Pencils
BABU: DAGGER, Pig mask
HEATHER: Purse
MISSY: Pass key on chair around neck

ACT I INTERMISSION:
Re-dress Georgie's bellhop costume in shredded
　　balloons and feathers
Remake bedspread
Guest - Set makeup for bomb explosion

SOUND EFFECTS

Shower Running
Offstage Crashbox
Swan Lake Valse
Bomb Explosion

SPECIAL EFFECTS

1) The helium-balloon flight at end of Act One was rigged on a pulley system above the US windows, the balloons masked the rope from which Georgie hung as he was pulled across the skyline of NY. Use two separate clusters of balloons. One rigged to the gag and one for the onstage prop attached to the service cart.

2) To rip hair out of Wally's head use matching crepe hair, kept in Georgie's pants pocket and palmed as Babu grabs him with the dagger.

3) Bedspread: Make bedspread with unsnappable panels to extend a full-size bed into a king-size bed.

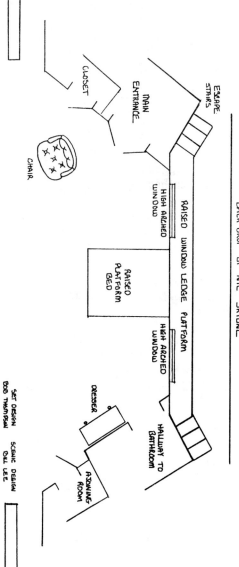

BACK DROP OF NYC SKYLINE

ESCAPE STAIRS

MAIN ENTRANCE

CLOSET

CHAIR

HIGH ARCHED WINDOW

RAISED WINDOW LEDGE PLATFORM

RAISED PLATFORM BED

HIGH ARCHED WINDOW

HALLWAY TO BATHROOM

DRESSER

ADJOINING ROOM

SET DESIGN
BOB THOMPSON

SCENIC DESIGN
BILL LEE

Going Ape

NICK HALL

(Little Theatre.) Farce.
3 male, 2 female—Interior

This hilarious and almost indescribable farce has some serious undertones. Rupert, an idealistic and romantic young orphan, has come to his uncle's house to commit suicide. This proves to be no easy matter. For one thing he is constantly attended by his uncle's attractive nurse/secretary. He is also constantly interrupted by a stream of visitors, at first fairly normal, but increasingly incredible. Rupert realizes that all the visitors are the same three people, and his attention is drawn toward understanding the preposterously Victorian plot in which he is trapped, and which, in a startlingly theatrical climax, he begins to understand. "An intricate plot with subtle foreshadowing and a grab bag of surprises . . . some of the funniest characters you'll ever see molded into a tight dramatic package."—News, Fort Myers. "Every scene transcends not only the imagination, but melds into a literally death-defying whole. It's fast, like 2,000 mph . . . a play as old and as contemporary as today." Sarasota Journal. "Going Ape is truly zany . . . the wackiness is infectious." —Time.

Eat Your Heart Out

NICK HALL

(Little Theatre.) Comedy.
3 male, 2 female—Interior

In this theatrical comedy Charlie, an out of work actor currently employed as a waiter, takes the audience through a sequence of hilarious encounters in a succession of Manhattan restaurants. By changing the tablecloths during the course of the action the basic setting of three tables and six chairs becomes a variety of New York restaurants, both elegant and shabby. The scenes change, the action is uninterrupted and the comedy never stops. The other performers play several parts: the girl desperately trying to eat snails and oysters to please her fiance; the middle-aged couple whose marriage is breaking up; the lovers so intent on each other they cannot order dinner; the rich, embittered astrologer; the timid man who never gets a waiter; the agents, directors, actors, and waiters. An amusing gallery of characters whose stories intertwine and finally involve Charlie. The author of "Accommodations" has written a very funny, contemporary play that is also a serious comedy of back-stage life. ". . . a sharp, stunning play. It'll make you howl—but better yet, it might even make you sniffle a bit."—Fort Lauderdale News. "Tightly written and very, very entertaining. I recommend it enthusiastically."—Miami Herald. ". . . About as good as anything I've ever seen in dinner theater . . ."—Fort Lauderdale Times.

Other Publications for Your Interest

THE MAN WITH THE PLASTIC SANDWICH

(LITTLE THEATRE—COMEDY)

By ROGER KARSHNER

2 men, 2 women—Simple exterior

Walter Price, a "basic blue" individual, is thrown out of work after twenty years with the same firm. During an anxiety-laden period of job hunting and readjustment Walter attempts to find solace on a bench in an urban park. Here he is confronted by three engaging, provocative characters. First there is Ellie, a high-spirited ingenue who represents hope; then Haley, a distinguished hobo representing wisdom; and finally Lenore, a hooker who represents reality. Each encounter enlightens Walter, gives him perspective, and ultimately new purpose and direction. A very funny play with bittersweet moments and three dimensional characters. "You will laugh until your sides feel as if they will burst, until your eyes begin to water, until you are sure that one more clever line or witty exchange will send you into a laughing fit from which you may never recover."—Chicago Sun-Times. "This play is truly high comedy and I can't think of a soul who wouldn't love the off-beat characters portrayed in this 4-spoked comedic wheel."—Chicago Reporter/Progress Newspapers.

THE DREAM CRUST

(LITTLE THEATRE—DRAMA)

By ROGER KARSHNER

3 men, 3 women, 1 10-year-old boy —Interior

Named in the Bruns-Mantle Yearbook as one of America's Best Plays. Frank Haynes, an earth-loving farmer, has given up his hound-dogging and high times under the pressure of the family's admonition that "A man has got to get ahead." Haynes would be happy to do nothing but tend his farm and reap whatever profit it might generate. But he realizes that there are five mouths depending on him and the lure of big money available to him in a nearby big-city factory too great to ignore. Set against a backdrop of the land-locked Midwest, the play dramatizes a man's persistent, agonizing search for personal freedom and the sense of loss between father and son. "A moving portrait of a land-locked family that needs to be seen."—Variety. "The plays' spirit, its underlying warmth, particularly in the unspoken father-son relationship, creates a world that's identifiable and that breathes."—L.A. Herald-Examiner.

SOCIAL SECURITY

(LITTLE THEATRE—COMEDY)

By ANDREW BERGMAN

3 men, 3 women—Interior

This is a real, honest-to-goodness hit Broadway comedy, as in the Good Old Days of Broadway. Written by one of Hollywood's top comedy screenwriters (''Blazing Saddles'' and ''The Inlaws'') and directed by the great Mike Nichols, this hilarious comedy starred Marlo Thomas and Ron Silver as a married couple who are art dealers. Their domestic tranquility is shattered upon the arrival of the wife's goody-goody nerd of a sister, her up-tight CPA husband and her Archetypal Jewish Mother. They are there to try to save their college student daughter from the horrors of living only for sex. The comic sparks really begin to fly when the mother hits it off with the elderly minimalist artist who is the art dealers' best client! ''Just when you were beginning to think you were never going to laugh again on Broadway, along comes *Social Security* and you realize, with a rising feeling of joy, that it is once more safe to giggle in the streets. Indeed, you can laugh out loud, joyfully, with, as it were, social security, for the play is a hoot, and better yet, a sophisticated, even civilized hoot.''—NY Post.   (#21255)

ALONE TOGETHER

(LITTLE THEATRE—COMEDY)

By LAWRENCE ROMAN

4 men, 2 women—Interior

Remember those wonderful Broadway comedies of the fifties and sixties, such as *Never Too Late* and *Take Her, She's Mine*? This new comedy by the author of *Under the Yum Yum Tree* is firmly in that tradition. Although not a hit with Broadway's jaded critics, *Alone Together* was a delight with audiences. On Broadway Janis Paige and Kevin McCarthy played a middle aged couple whose children have finally left the nest. They are now alone together—but not for long. All three sons come charging back home after experiencing some Hard Knocks in the Real World—and Mom and Dad have quite a time pushing them out of the house so they can once again be *alone together*. ''Mr. Roman is a fast man with a funny line.''—Chr. Sci. Mon. ''A charmer.''—Calgary Sunday Sun. ''An amiable comedy . . . the audience roared with recognition, pleasure and amusement.''—Gannett Westchester Newsp. ''Delightfully wise and witty.'' Hollywood Reporter. ''One of the funniest shows we've seen in ages.''—Herald-News. TV.   (#238)

Other Publications for Your Interest

MOVIE OF THE MONTH
(COMEDY)

By DANIEL MELTZER

2 men—Interior

This new comedy by the author of the ever-popular *The Square Root of Love* is an amusing satire of commercial television. B.S., a TV programming executive, is anxious to bolster his network's ratings, which have been sagging of late due to programming disasters such as a documentary called "The Ugly Truth" (says B.S.: "What the hell is The Ugly Truth, and how the hell did it get into our Prime Time?") His eagerbeaver assistant, appropriately named Broun, has found a script which he is sure can be made into a hit "Movie of the Month". It's about this Danish prince, see, who comes home from college to find that his uncle has murdered his father and married his mother . . . Well, naturally, B.S. has his own ideas about how to fix such a totally unbelievable plot . . .   (#17621)

SUNDANCE
(ALL GROUPS—COMEDY)

By MEIR Z. RIBALOW

5 men—Simple interior

This new comedy from the author of *Shrunken Heads* is set in a sort of metaphysical wild west saloon. The characters include Hickock, Jesse, the Kid, and the inevitable Barkeep. Hickock kills to uphold the law. Jesse kills for pleasure. The Kid kills to bring down The Establishment. What if, wonders the Barkeep, they met up with the Ultimate Killer—who kills for no reason, who kills simply because that's what he does? Enter Sundance. He does not kill to uphold the law, for pleasure, or to make a political statement, or because he had a deprived childhood. And he proceeds to kill everyone, exiting at the end with his sixguns blazing! "Witty, strong, precise, unusually well-written."—The Guardian. "A brilliant piece."—Dublin Evening Press. This co-winner of the 1981 Annual NYC Metropolitan Short Play Festival has been a success in 6 countries!   (#3113)

SAMUEL FRENCH has:
AMERICA'S
FAVORITE COMEDIES

ABSURD PERSON SINGULAR – ACCOMMODATIONS – ANGEL ON MY SHOULDER – BAREFOOT IN THE PARK – A BEDFULL OF FOREIGNERS – BEDROOM – FARCE – BUTTERFLIES ARE FREE – CACTUS FLOWER – CALIFORNIA SUITE – CHAMPAGNE COMPLEX – CHAPTER TWO – CHARLIE'S AUNT – A COUPLA WHITE CHICKS – DON'T DRINK THE WATER – THE DREAM CRUST – FLING! – FOOLS – THE FOURPOSTER – THE GIN GAME – THE GINGERBREAD LADY – GOD'S FAVORITE THE GOOD DOCTOR – HERE LIES JEREMY TROY – I OUGHT TO BE IN PICTURES – THE IMPOSSIBLE YEARS – IN ONE BED . . . AND OUT THE OTHER – IT HAD TO BE YOU – KINDLING – THE LADY WHO CRIED FOX – LOVE, SEX AND THE I.R.S. – LOVERS AND OTHER STRANGERS – LUNCH HOUR – THE MARRIAGE-GO-ROUND

For descriptions of plays, consult our Basic Catalogue of Plays.